THE BRIDE OF
Anguished English

Also by Richard Lederer

Basic Verbal Skills (with Philip Burnham)

Anguished English

Get Thee to a Punnery

Crazy English

The Play of Words

The Miracle of Language

More Anguished English

Adventures of a Verbivore

Literary Trivia (with Michael Gilleland)

Building Bridge (with Bo Schambelan and Arnold Fisher)

Nothing Risqué, Nothing Gained

The Write Way (with Richard Dowis)

Pun & Games

Fractured English

The Word Circus

Sleeping Dogs Don't Lay (with Richard Dowis)

Anguished English

A Bonus of Bloopers, Blunders, Botches, and Boo-Boos

Richard Lederer

Illustrations by Jim McLean

St. Martin's Press ❧ New York

Illustrations © 2000 by Jim McLean

www.stmartins.com

Book design by Ellen Cipriano

LIBRARY OF CONGRESS CATALOGING-IN-PUBLICATION DATA
Lederer, Richard.
The bride of anguished English : a bonus of bloopers, blunders, botches, and boo-boos/Richard Lederer ; illustrations by Jim McLean.—1st ed.
p. cm.
ISBN 0-312-26223-X
1. English language—Errors of usage—Humor. I. Title.
PN6231.E74 L418 2000
428'.002'07—dc21   00-031740

First Edition: October 2000

10 9 8 7 6 5 4 3 2 1

To Joan van Egeren,
mother of the bride

Contents

A World of Errors

Press Messes

How's That Again?

Grammar Gremlins

Introduction

Although my name appears on the cover of this book, I am not truly the author. *The Bride of Anguished English* was created by legions of oldsters and youngsters around the world who fabricate wacky words, lacerated lingo, ridiculous rhetoric, ditzy diction, fractured phrases, idiotic idioms, lipslips, muddled modifiers, mixed-up metaphors, and skewed syntax. None of these people is a relative of yours, of course.

For this book I have simply acted as a relentless hunter-gatherer of other people's verbal vagaries, which I have organized into catchy categories. I have attempted to accumulate the most tee-hee collection of nutty nouns, vagrant verbs, mangled modifiers, and preposterous prepositions this side of *Webster's Unabridged*. Each and every item is genuine, certified, and authentic. None was invented by this delighted compiler.

I have kept the editing to the barest minimum in order to preserve the integrity of the original goofs and gaffes. I wouldn't dream of changing a single word of bloopers, blunders, botches, and boo-boos like these:

• A trainer explained to the athletes under his care, "I am not opposed to high spirits after a game, but when it comes to spreading tacks around the locker room floor, I really must put my foot down."

• In a restaurant, a customer asked a waitress for chicken soup. Later the patron changed his mind and decided to order pea soup. The waitress yelled to the cook, "Hold the chicken. Make it pea!"

• A man informed his wife, "The gynecologist's office called, and your Pabst Beer is normal."

• A woman went to the post office to buy stamps for her Christmas cards. "What denomination?" asked the clerk. "Oh, good heavens! Have we come to this?" said the woman. "Well, give me 50 Baptist and 50 Catholic ones."

• An educational publisher had to recall shipments of pencils bearing the antidrug slogan "Too Cool to Do Drugs." The recall was prompted by a fourth-grader, who pointed out to the company that, when sharpened, the pencils read successively, "Cool to Do Drugs" and "Do Drugs."

• After being served matzo ball soup three days in a row, a woman asked, "Isn't there any other part of the matzo you can eat?"

To the unknowing contributors to *The Bride of Anguished English* I offer my profound gratitude for improving the health of the readers of this book. More and more experts have come to acknowledge that laughter is as important to our health as medicine and bandages. More and more hospitals, nursing homes, and rehabilitation centers now bring in clowns, provide "humor carts" to distribute funny books and videos, or send patients to "humor rooms" for daily doses of jokes and laughter.

"Humor undoubtedly has a positive health benefit," says Steve Sultanoff, a California psychologist and president of the American Association for Therapeutic Humor. "It changes our emotional state, our perspective on life, and, through laughter, our physiological state."

India also considers laughter the best medicine. Members of Bombay's twenty-eight chapters of Laughing Club International congregate in parks every morning and practice. They start with a few chuckles and then let them develop into knee-slapping laughter. Club members claim that laughter expands the lungs, colors the cheeks, reduces blood pressure, tones the muscles, strengthens the immune system, multiplies endorphins, and alleviates bronchitis and asthma.

Did you know that babies are born with certain natural instincts? Neurologists have discovered that the reason they cry right after birth is that they instinctively understand the amount of the national debt they are going to be saddled with.

Just kidding. But I'm completely serious when I report the fact that five-year-olds naturally laugh about 250 times a day. How sad it is that as we age, we almost inevitably gain girth and lose mirth. Many of us don't laugh 250 times *a month*. That's why I hope that my anthologies of accidental atrocities will help people get back in touch with their innate sense of humor. That goal has been validated by the scores of testimonials I have received about the healing power of laughing at bloopers:

• You don't want to be caught reading books like yours in a public place, unless you don't mind making a fool of yourself, especially in airplanes. Certain behavior is treated with a great deal of suspicion when you're 30,000 feet in the air.
—*Maggie Valentine Inskeep, Greeley, Colorado*

• After reading Richard Lederer's student bloopers, I have decided to ask my attorney to file suit for cruel and unusual laughter. Furthermore, since distributing copies to selected friends in my retirement home, we have decided to file a class-action suit, if we can determine which class we're in.
—*Annie Mae Turner, Montgomery, Alabama*

• Two years ago I gave birth to child number three. As part of some informative survey, the nurse asked me a number of questions, during the labor process, for the hospital's poll.
One of the questions was "How do you handle stress?" My answer (in between contractions) was "I take a bubble bath with Richard Lederer." My husband, of course, knew what I meant by such a statement, but it caught the nurse off guard. That should teach them to wait until after the baby is born before asking such survey questions!
I also use your writing as an antidepressant. You are much cheaper than Prozac and without so many side effects!
—*Ruthie Oberg, Oskaloosa, Iowa*

• More than four years ago you helped my children and me through a difficult time. We lived in the San Fernando Valley area of Los Angeles close to the epicenter of the 1994 Northridge earthquake. Our home was severely damaged, and we ended up sleeping in the hallway for the three weeks it took for us to be able to move so that repairs could begin.

Aftershocks were constant. The situation was stressful, to say the least. But we had your books *Crazy English* and *Anguished English*. In the evenings, we would all huddle in the hall and read the books aloud and laugh like crazy people. So thank you for helping us maintain our humor and what little sanity we had left.

—*Sandy Roberts, Sherman Oaks, California*

The President's Council on Humor Fitness requires me to state that the bloopers served up in this book are certified, fast acting, and fat free. They are absolutely pure and contain no artificial additives or preservatives. No animals were harmed in the capture and exhibiting of these beastly blunders.

Active ingredients in these slips of the tongue and slops of the pen include humor, healing, nourishment, and verbal fiber. The contents of these pages are unconditionally guaranteed to supply the recommended daily dose of grins, giggles, and guffaws. And *The Bride of Anguished English* is so cool, it needs no refrigeration.

"Laughter is the jam on the toast of life. It adds flavor, keeps it from being too dry, and makes it easier to swallow," writes Diane Johnson. May this pleasury of bloopers make your life even more delicious—tastier, sweeter, spicier, juicier, even meatier—and a lot easier to swallow. If you would like to contribute to the next feast of flubbery, please send your most super-duper bloopers to richard.lederer@pobox.com. Show me the bloopers!

Richard Lederer
9974 Scripps Ranch Blvd.
#201
San Diego, CA 92131

pobox.com/~verbivore

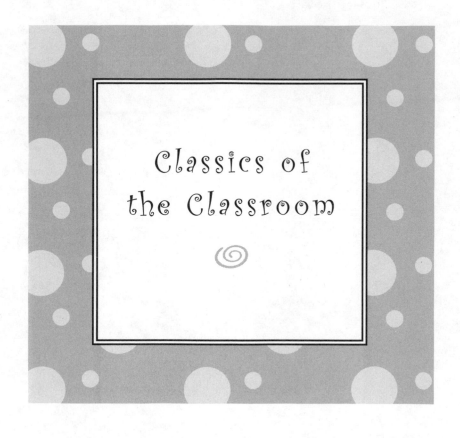

Classics of
the Classroom

"My name begins with the letter 'M,' and I pick things up. What am I?"
"You're a mother."

We Kid You Not

The sins of the fathers, the Second Commandment tells us, shall be visited upon the children unto the third and fourth generations. And so shall the fluffs and flubs and goofs and gaffes of the fathers (and mothers), albeit in a much more innocent form. Children are rich natural sources of fresh bloopers. Some of the brightest pearls in my collection fall from the mouths of babes who are scarcely older than babies.

For example, an eight-year-old girl submitted this gem about "people" to her teacher:

People are composed of girls and boys, also men and women.
Boys are no good at all until they grow up and get married. Men

who don't get married are no good either. Boys are an awful bother. They want everything they see except soap.

My ma is a woman and my pa is a man. A woman is a grown-up girl with children. My pa is such a nice man that I think he must have been a girl when he was a little boy.

Schoolteachers love adding such writing to their collections of "kiddisms" and keep journals of the amusing things their students have said. Some send these slops of the pen and slips of the lips to me so that I can share them with you:

• A nursery-school teacher had spent half an hour dressing her kiddies for their outdoor playtime, pulling on boots, zipping and buttoning coats, matching mittens and gloves. As she finished struggling with Jennifer's boots, she let out a sigh of relief. Then Jennifer tugged on her arm and announced, "These boots aren't mine, Teacher."

With a groan the teacher knelt down and pulled off the boots. "Do you know whose boots these are, Jennifer?"

"Sure. They're my sister's. Mom makes me wear them anyway."

• On the first day of school, the kindergarten teacher said, "If anyone has to go to the bathroom, hold up two fingers."

A little voice from the back of the room asked, "How will that help?"

• A third-grader announced that he had been to an upholstery farm. "What?" he was asked, and again he said that he had visited an upholstery farm. When asked to explain what he had seen there, he said, "Why, turkeys and chickens, of course."

• A teacher was giving a lesson on the circulation of the blood. Trying to make the matter clearer, he said, "Now, boys and girls, if I stood on my head, the blood, as you know, would run into it, and I would turn red in the face."

"Yes, sir," the students agreed.

"Then why is it that while I am standing upright in the ordinary position, the blood doesn't run into my feet?"

A little fellow shouted, "'Cause your feet ain't empty."

• The kindergarten teacher was showing her class an encyclopedia page picturing several national flags. She pointed to the American flag and asked, "What flag is this?"

A little girl called out, "That's the flag of our country."

"Very good," the teacher said. "And what is the name of our country?"

" 'Tis of thee," the girl said confidently.

• During academic practice, students were asked to name our national anthem. One student answered, "The Star-Strangled Banner."

• "Does anyone know what a pasture is?" asked the fourth-grade teacher.

A hand shot up, and a pupil volunteered, "He's the guy at church!"

"No," corrected a classmate. "The guy at church isn't called a pasture. He's called a miniature."

• When a six-year-old was presented with a photograph of a mummy and was asked what a mummy is, he replied, "A mummy is a dead person wrapped in toilet paper."

• Miss Mayfield had been giving her second-grade students a lesson on science. She had explained about magnets and showed how they could pick up nails and other bits of iron. Now it was question time, and she asked, "My name begins with the letter 'M,' and I pick things up. What am I?"

A little boy in the front row said, "You're a mother."

Who else but a mother (except, on occasion, a father) picks up things so thoroughly? And who else but a mother picks up and records the darndest things that kids say?:

• A mother was putting away dishes in the kitchen when she heard her son call from the den, "Mom, come quickly. I learned how to make babies in school today."

She almost dropped the dishes and had just composed herself when he again called, "Mom, come and see what I learned about making babies."

When she finally arrived, her son beamed enthusiastically and said, "See, Mom, you can change the y to i and add es to make *babies*."

• A mother was pleased with the card her son had made her for Christmas but was puzzled as to the scraggly-looking tree from which many presents dangled. From the very top hung something that looked strangely like a bullet. She asked him if he would explain the drawing and why the tree itself was so bare, instead of a fat and bushy pine tree. "It's not a Christmas tree," he said. "It's a cartridge in a pear tree."

• A four-year-old girl was having a hard time grasping the concept of marriage. Her mother took out the wedding album, thinking visual images would help, and explained the entire service to her daughter. Once finished, Mother asked if the little girl had any questions, and the tike replied, "Oh, I see. Is that when Mommy came to work for us?"

• Grandma decided to find out if her granddaughter had learned her colors yet. She pointed out object after object and asked the child what color each one was. Granddaughter answered each challenge correctly. Grandma was having so much fun that she continued. Finally, the child headed for the door and, pursing her lips, said, "Grandma, I think you should try to figure out some of these yourself!"

• A mother took her four-year-old son to a friend's birthday party, where the father of the birthday boy had rented a cotton-candy machine for the day. The visiting child refused to try any cotton candy, whimpering, "Mommy, you shouldn't eat insulation!"

• Another four-year-old boy was out in his backyard when he noticed a friend of his mother smoking a cigarette.

"What are you doing?" asked the tike.

"Smoking," explained the grown-up.

To which the child replied, "Don't you know that if you keep doing that you'll get canceled?"

• A three-year-old boy went with his dad to see a litter of kittens. On returning home, he breathlessly informed his mother, "There were two boy kittens and two girl kittens."

"How did you know?" his mother asked.

"Daddy picked them up and looked underneath," he replied. "I think it's printed on the bottom."

• Another three-year-old put his shoes on by himself. His mother noticed the left was on the right foot. She said, "Son, your shoes are on the wrong feet."

He looked up at her with a raised brow and said, "Don't kid me, Mom. I *know* they're my feet."

• A mother and her young son returned from the grocery store and began putting away the groceries. The boy opened the box of animal crackers and spread them all over the table.

"What are you doing?" his mother asked.

"The box says you can't eat them if the seal is broken," the boy explained. "I'm looking for the seal."

• Mother (to her six-year-old son): What sound does a cow make?

Son: Moo.

Mother: What sound does a duck make?

Son: Quack, Quack.

Mother: You're such a smart little boy. Can you tell me what sound a frog makes?

Son (after hesitating): Bud. Lite.

• A little boy was upset with himself. When his grandfather asked him what was the matter, he spluttered, "Gramps, I wrote down the wrong homework assignment and spent the whole evening studying something I didn't have to know until next week!"

• A mother was telling her little girl what her own childhood was like: "We used to skate outside on a pond. I had a swing made from a tire. It hung from a tree in our front yard. We rode our pony. We picked wild raspberries in the woods."

The little girl was wide-eyed, taking this in. At last she said, "I sure wish I'd gotten to know you sooner!"

• A little girl was diligently pounding away on her father's word processor. She told him she was writing a story. "What's it about?" he asked.

"I don't know," she replied. "I can't read."

• "Do you want a boy or a girl?" an adult asked the little boy about his mother's pregnancy. Parroting the proverbial answer he had so often heard from his parents, he replied, "We don't care if it's a boy or a girl, just as long as it's wealthy."

• Lisa was now seven and took a special pride in her growing vocabulary. Referring to an American history lesson, she announced, "We learned about the American Constipation, Mommy."

- When her mother's sister appeared at the door, a little girl exclaimed, "Ooh, Auntie. I'm so glad you've arrived 'cause Daddy said your visit today was just what we needed!"
- A little boy found the old family Bible and started thumbing through the pages. As he was turning the yellowed pages, a pressed tree leaf fell out. Wide-eyed, he exclaimed, "Hey, this must be where Adam and Eve left their clothes!"
- A small boy wrote in a Christmas card to his aunt, "And I want to thank you for all the presents you have sent in the past, as well as all the ones you are going to send me this Christmas."
- A new neighbor asked the little girl next door if she had any brother and sisters. She replied, "No, I'm the lonely child."
- Hurrying to get his morning off to a good start, a young father was surprised when his six-year-old son brought him a cup of freshly made coffee.

Delighted, he thanked the thoughtful youngster.

He realized, however, that he was drinking the worst cup of coffee he had ever tasted. With a forced, grateful smile, he finally reached the bottom of the cup, where he found a small, green, plastic army man.

Patiently he asked his son, "Why is there an army man in my coffee?"

Proudly his son responded, "Daddy, don't you listen to the man on TV? He says, 'The best part of waking up is soldiers in your cup'!"

Before continuing to read this book, please note the following warnings: Do not submerge *The Bride of Anguished English* in water. Remember that this book is not to be used as a flotation device and may be harmful if swallowed. Please discard if seal is broken. Do not share this book with others without warning them of possible side effects, which may include uncontrollable laughter and tears.

Actually, tears of laughter have been proved to carry away toxins found in cells of people under stress. These tears differ from those produced from an irritant to the eye, such as when cutting an onion. May you shed many a tear of laughter as you trip the light fantastic humor of this book.

THE KIDDISMS HALL OF FAME

- Auntie, the gray in your hair makes you look very extinguished.
- One day I will enter Pooh-Bear-ty.
- We're watching the story of E.T., the Extra Cholesterol.
- [Looking at twins in a baby carriage]: There's the baby—and there's the co-baby!
- Everybody should try to have a grandmother, especially if you don't have television, because grandmothers are the only grown-ups who have got time.

When in the course of...

*Benjamin Franklin and Thomas Jefferson were two singers
of the Decoration of Independence.*

American History According to Student Bloopers

Citizens of the United States can be divided into two groups. The first is composed of people who speak and write English clearly, crisply, concisely, and communicatively. I shall not mention them again in this book—and, frankly, I'm not sure that they really exist.

The other group is composed of people who fudge their facts, mix their metaphors, confuse their clichés, slaughter their syntax, and dangle their participles in public. These are the happily unaware, whose inter-pretations are unclouded by doubt. These are the people who create the mangled meanderings that Funk would never tell Wagnall and that Merriam would never confide to Webster.

These citizens of America start fracturing at an early age, as young scholars in our nation's schools. Witness this fractured chronicle of American history composed entirely of certified, genuine, authentic, un-retouched student fabrications. Not a one, of course, was written by a child of yours:

Christopher Columbus discovered America while cursing about the Atlantic Ocean. Little did he know that he had just begun history!

His ships were named the Nina, the Pinta Colada, and the Santa Fe. Columbus knelt, thanked God, and put the American flag in the ground. Tarzan is a short name for the American flag. Its full name is the Tarzans and Stripes.

Later, Jamestown was discovered by King James the One and named after him. King James persuaded the Queen to give him the land, and he sent a gang of settlers over here in 1607.

The Pilgrims crossed the ocean in hardships. This was called the Pill's Grim Progress. These people always wore old shoes with a big buckle on the top of them. The men wore pants that only came a little ways past their knees, and the girls wore funny bonnets.

The winter of 1620 was a hard one for the settlers. Many people died, and many babies were born. Captain John Smith was responsible for all this. The Pilgrims appointed Thanksgiving, and it soon became a national holiday all over the world.

One of the causes of the Revolutionary War was the English put tacks in their tea. The Boston Tea Party wasn't what we would think of if we thought of a tea party. It was a raid where they threw all the tea into Boston Harbor, which they all drank. Also, the colonists would send their parcels through the post without stamps. Paul Revere's Ride wasn't as famous as some people make it. He had to have the help of Longfellow on it. Mr. Revere started his famous ride in Lexington, which is in Philadelphia, and paddled by canew to Boston. Then he rode through the streets yelling, "Too warm! Too warm! The Red Colts are coming!"

During the Revolutionary War, the Red Coats and Paul Revere were throwing balls over stone walls. The dogs were barking, and the peacocks crowing. Finally, General Corn Wallace surrendered, and the war was over. When General Burgundy surrendered to Sara's Toga, the colonists won the war and no longer had to pay for taxis.

America was founded by four fathers. Delegates from the original 13 states formed the Contented Congress. Benjamin Franklin and Thomas Jefferson, a Virgin, were two singers of the Decoration of Independence, which says that all men are cremated equal and are well endowed by their creator. John Hancott signed first because he was president and a very heavy man.

Franklin had gone to Boston carrying all his clothes in his pocket and a loaf of bread under each arm. He invented electricity by rubbing two cats backwards and declared, "A horse divided against itself cannot stand!" Franklin died in 1790 and is still dead.

George Washington led the United States to what it is today, while Ben and Dick Arnold were terrible traitors. Washington crossed the Delaware River, married Martha Custis, and in due time became the Father of Our Country. The difference between a king and a president is that a king is the son of his father, but a president isn't. Washington was a very social man. He had big balls, and everyone enjoyed them. His farewell address was Mount Vernon.

Soon the Constitution of the United States was adopted to secure domestic hostility. Under the Constitution, the people have the right to bare arms. After the Constitution was finished, Washington and Franklin added the bill for rice.

Mexico was conquered by Kotex. De Soto was one of the cruelest conquerors there ever was. When Indians got in his way, he just ran right over them. That's probably why they named a car after him.

In the middle of the 18th century, all the morons moved to

Utah. In the early 19th century, Lois and Clark explored the Louisiana Purchase. They became well-known all over the world and in foreign countries. Traveling by stagecoach in the Old West was dangerous because you had a good chance of being stopped by bandits and being robed and plungered. The two greatest marshals of the Old West were Wyatt Burp and Wild Bill Hiccup. General George Custer extinguished himself at the Battle of the Little Big Horn.

Abraham Lincoln became America's greatest precedent. Lincoln's mother died in infancy, and he was born in a log cabin which he built with his very own hands. When Lincoln was president, he wore only a tall silk hat. He said, "In onion there is strength."

Lincoln was president during the Civil War. Matthew Brady, a filmer, took a picture of it. The Civil War was started by John Brown, a rabbit abolitionist, and Harriet Bitcher Stowe, who wrote Uncle Tom's Cabinet. They caused the Southern states to succeed. After the Civil War, General Lou Wallace wrote Gone with the Wind and Bend Her.

Abraham Lincoln wrote the Gettysburg Address while traveling from Washington to Gettysburg on the back of an envelope. He spoke at the dedication of a dormitory for the wounded soldiers who died at Gettysburg.

He also freed the slaves by signing the Emaciation Proclamation. Lincoln debated John Kennedy in 1960. Kennedy won because he looked better than Lincoln, who had pallor due to his assassination.

On the night of April 14, 1865, Lincoln went to the theater and got shot in his seat by one of the actors in a moving picture show. At first, the president's wife didn't take notice of him slumped over in her lap. She thought he had just snoozed off as usual. The believed assinator was John Wilkes Booth, a supposingly insane actor. This ruined Booth's career.

The 19th century was a time of a great many thoughts and inventions. People stopped reproducing by hand and started reproducing by machine. The invention of the steamboat by Robert

Fulton caused a network of rivers to spring up. Samuel Morse invented a code of telepathy. Eli Whitney invented the spinning gin. Thomas Edison invented the pornograph and the indecent lamp. Macaroni invented the wireless telephone. Andrew Carnegie started the steal business. Goethals dug the alimentary canal. And Cyrus McCormick invented the McCormick Raper, which did the work of a hundred men.

The First World War was caused by the assignation of the Arch-Duck by an anahist. During the early part of World War I, President Woodrow Wilson urged the people to stay in neutral. He brought up the League of Nations, but it never did much except write a lot of letters, declare war on people, and try to beat peace into them. Then Wilson had many foreign affairs, and America entered the war. The unfortunate soldiers spent day after day up to their wastes in filth.

World War I made people so sad that it brought on the Great Depression. Then the New Deal tried to make sure that the stock market will never happen again.

Charles Limburger was the first man to ever cross the Atlantic alone. He wanted to go by regular airlines, but he couldn't afford to buy a ticket. When he got to Paris, all the French people shouted, "Bonzai!"

World War II happened when Adolph Hitler and the Knotsies had erotic dreams of conquest all over Europe. Hitler always liked to call himself Der Furor, but his real name was Messer Smith.

Franklin Roosevelt won a landslide and went over there and put a stop to Hitler, who committed suicide in his bunk. We dropped the atomic bomb on Kamakazi, a heavy industrious city, and three days later on Nicaragua. Finally, World War II ended on VD Day.

Martin Luther had a dream. He went to Washington and recited his Sermon on the Monument. Later, he nailed 96 Protestants in the Watergate Scandal, which ushered in a new error in the anals of human history.

THE HISTORY BLOOPERS HALL OF FAME

- Early Egyptian women often wore a garment called a calasiris. It was a sheer dress which started beneath the breasts which hung to the floor.
- The Greeks invented three kinds of columns—corynthian, ironic, and dorc.
- William Tell shot an arrow through an apple while standing on his son's head.
- Life during the Middle Ages was especially difficult for the pheasants.
- Sir Francis Drake circumcised the world with a 100-foot clipper.

The soothsayer warned Julius Caesar to beware the Eyes of March.

Schoolishness

A boy came home from school with his exam results. "What did you get?" asked his father.

"My marks are under water," said the boy.

"What do you mean 'under water'?"

"They're all below 'C' level."

Striving for vocabulary growth, a teacher asked his students, "What is the opposite of sadness?"

"Joy," volunteered Marjorie.

"And the opposite of depression, Billy?"

"Elation."

"And you, Clem, how about the opposite of woe?"

"I believe that would be *giddy up*."

Those two anecdotes are made-up, but the real-life answers that students commit to test papers often keep students' grades below 'C' level, in a state of woe:

What is the capital of Italy?

I!

Why did the London theaters close between 1592 and 1594?

Because of the Dark Ages. There was no light to be able to watch the play at night.

Characterize Henry VII and Henry VIII.

Henry VII and Henry VIII were two-door kings.

What is Alzheimer's?

Imported beer.

Who is Louis Armstrong?

The first man on the moon.

Who was Count Basie?

A vampire.

Students often revise history, geography, and literature beyond recognition. While scribbling away in an exam room, students often conjure up facts and events that have never existed. The blunders, bloopers, boo-boos, botches, bungles, and boners you are about to read were cheerfully committed by students and scholars all around the world. These classroom classics prove that, as one student penned in a composition, "Adolescence is that time in life between puberty and adultery":

• No human beings were around during the Ice Age because it was the pre-stork era.

• The Greeks, with the help of the messy Potamians, invented history. The Greeks were a happy lot. They were always running races, throwing things, and jumping over things. This caused them to invent the marathon.

• The Acropolis of Athens contained the Parthion, the Erectum, and the Esophagus, a temple to the war god.

• In the *Iliad*, written by Homer, great worriers battle for honor, treasures, and women.

- Queen Dildo was impaled into a world of madness.
- The greatest evacuations the world has ever known were made by Schliemann on the site of Troy.
- Cleopatra died when an ass bit her.
- The soothsayer warned Julius Caesar to beware the Eyes of March. Brutus killed Caesar because he was an ego testicle man. Caesar's last sentence was "Eat you, Brutus!"
- Beowulf suckled Uncle Remus and his brother who founded Rome.
- Menstrual shows were popular during the medieval period.
- One of the wives of Henry VIII was named Anne of Cleavage.
- The Protestant reformation came about when Martin Luther had too many papal bulls and too few bowel movements.
- Romeo saw Juliet for the first time at the massacred ball. Then they secretly married.
- Macbeth became Thane of Candor. Lady Macbeth felt her quilt in Act V.
- In Shakespeare's *A Midsummer Night's Dream*, Puck turns Bottom's head into an ass.
- Oliver Cromwell had a large red nose, but under it were deeply religious feelings.
- The French Revolution took place because Louis XIV was revolting.
- Robinson Crusoe was shipwrecked on the shores of an uninhibited island.
- Coleridge dealt with his problems by drinking himself into a Bolivian every night.
- Edgar Allan Poe was born in Boston in 1809 and was found unconscious. Three days later, he died in 1849.
- Charles Dickens left his wife after she had bored him with ten children.
- The ghost of Bob Marley visited Ebenezer Scrooge.
- During the Civil War, Abraham Lincoln had to memorize the Gettysburg Address.
- The general direction of the Alps is straight up.
- France is a major city in England. Its major export is French fries. Most of the houses in France are made of plaster of Paris.

- F. Scott Fitzgerald's *The Great Gatsby* exemplified American culture in the 1920s to a tea.

In the grand tradition of Doll Tearsheet and Mrs. Malaprop and the modern school of Dizzy Dean, Samuel Goldwyn, Yogi Berra, and Howard Cosell, young scholars around our nation manage to mangle the mother tongue with bizarre word choices:

- An actuary is a home for birds.
- In the United States, criminals are put to death by elocution.
- The police called 911 to get an ambulance to take him to the mortgage.
- In Venice the people travel around the canals on gorgonzolas.
- In England they have the custom of having tea and strumpets.
- During the 1920s, several films were released in two virgins: one silent and the other with sounds.
- A scout obeys all to whom obedience is due and respects all duly constipated authorities.
- The word *trousers* is an uncommon noun because it is singular at the top and plural at the bottom.
- A census taker is a man who goes from house to house increasing the population.
- Paul began life unfortunately. The doctor was not present at his conception.
- Married life and single life have many similarities and many in-differences.
- Refrain means don't do it. A refrain in music is the part you'd better not try to sing.
- Probably the most marvelous fugue was the one between the Hatfields and McCoys.
- My very best liked piece of music is the Bronze Lullaby.
- A trumpet is an instrument when it is not an elephant sound.
- The flute is a skinny-high shape-sounded instrument.
- Tubas are a bit too much.

Professor Henry Higgins's lament to Eliza Doolittle was "Why can't the English teach their children how to speak?" A parallel utterance from many parents is "Why can't the teachers teach my children how to write?" Or as one young scholar penned in an essay, "I have difficulty writing because I get abstracted."

THE STUDENT BLOOPERS HALL OF FAME

- In 1957, Eugene O'Neill won a Pullet Surprise.
- Romeo's last wish was to be laid by Juliet.
- Johann Sebastian Bach wrote a great many musical compositions and had a large number of children. In between, he practiced on an old spinster which he kept up in his attic.
- In the Middle Ages, people put on plays about ghosts, goblins, virgins, and other mythical creatures.
- When a boy and a girl are deeply in love, there is no quilt felt between them.

Liter

A liter is a lot of newborn puppies.

Weird Science

A second-grade teacher gathered her pupils in the Science Corner to review the five senses—sight, hearing, touch, taste, and smell.

"You forgot one of the senses," remarked one of her charges.

"Which is that?" asked his teacher.

And the child explained, "The sense of humor."

That sixth sense—the sense of humor—pervades the darnedest things that kids throughout our land write in science class. Billy, a first-grader, told his teacher that he had found a frog.

"Is the frog dead or alive?" asked the teacher.

"It's dead."

"How do you know?"

"I pissed in its ear."

"You what???"

And Billy said, "You know, I went to his ear and said, 'PSST!' and it didn't move. So it must be dead."

Recently, a number of school systems have undertaken initiatives to boost their students' knowledge of and scores in science. Nonetheless, science fantasy and science friction pervade student writing. It is truly brain boggling what havoc our young (and not so young) Einsteins can wreak on the field of scientific inquiry:

- A liter is a lot of newborn puppies.
- The equator is an imaginary lion that runs around the world forever.
- The atom is composed of protons and electricians.
- Geometry was invented by Eucalyptus.
- We do not raise silkworms in the United States, because we get our silk from rayon. He is a larger worm and gives more silk.
- Vacuums are nothings. We only mention them to let them know that we know they are there.
- Comets are made up of organic material, ice, and miscellaneous gases and are thought to be ruminants from the beginning of the universe.
- An optimist is a doctor who looks after your eyes. A pessimist is one who attends to your feet.
- A canal is a small stream of water made by man.
- Dew is formed on leaves when the sun shines down on them and makes them perspire.
- One of the main causes of dust is janitors.
- One by-product of raising cattle is calves.
- We know that Bigfoot exists because we have seen his droppings. They are human shaped.
- The pineapple is the chief product of the pine tree.
- Rotation of crops is so that they can get the sun on all sides.
- Space is the final front tear.
- A fossil is an extinct animal. The older it is, the more extinct it gets.

- American time is behind British time because America was discovered later.
- The Earth needs the O-Zone layer to keep in the gravity.
- The climate is hottest next to the Creator.
- The tides are a fight between the Earth and the Moon. All water tends towards the Moon because there is no water on the Moon, and nature abhors a vacuum. I forget where the Sun joins in this fight.
- We say the cause of perfume disappearing is evaporation. Evaporation gets blamed for a lot of things people forget to put the top on.
- Thunder is a rich source of loudness.
- Wind is like air, only pushier.
- Water vapor gets together in a big cloud. When it gets big enough to be called a drop, it does.
- Mercury is the god of the weather because he is found in thermometers.
- Some people can tell the time by looking at the Sun, but I have never been able to make out the numbers.
- I am not sure how clouds get formed, but the clouds know how to do it, and that is the important thing.
- South America has cold summers and warm winters, but somehow they still manage.
- Most books say the Sun is a star. But it still knows how to change back into the Sun in the daytime.
- The hydrogen bomb is sometimes called the itch bomb. I don't know why.
- Many dead animals of the past changed into fossils while others preferred to be oil.
- Kangaroos are not mammals. They are menopausals.
- A planet cannot have an axis until it can get a line to run through it.
- Radio waves are very heavy. That's why they build those big towers. To hold them up.
- In spring, the salmon swim upstream to spoon.

The hygiene classrooms are far from immune to verbal schoolishness:

• Heredity means that if your grandfather didn't have any children, then your father probably wouldn't have any, and neither would you, probably.

• A skeleton is a man with his outside off and his inside sticking out.

• There are 26 vitamins in all, but some of the letters are yet to be discovered.

• To keep in good health, inhale and exhale once a day, and do gymnastics.

• I do not believe in premartial sex because he or she might get pregnut.

• In sex, men use a condom; women use a diagram.

• Gender is how you tell if a man is masculine, feminine, or neuter.

• An appendix is something you find in the back of a book. But if it gets in people, it has to be taken out.

• The blood circulates through the body by flowing down one leg and up the other.

• Natural immunity is catching a disease without the aid of a physician.

• The four seasons are salt, pepper, mustard, and vinegar.

• Mono sodium glue to mate enhances the flavor of food.

• I'll never forget the time my brother choked at dinner and my father gave him the Hemlock Remover.

• To guard against heart attacks, I need to get my castor oil levels checked.

• Green persimmons are a rich source of indigestion.

• People who go to see optimists often find that their eyes and headaches disappear.

• When you breathe, you inspire. When you do not breathe, you expire.

• An artery carries blood to or from the heart. I forget which. But the body remembers, and that's the important thing.

THE UNSCIENTIFIC HALL OF FAME

- Scientists are hypothetical people.
- Our new teacher told us all about fossils. Before she came to our class, I didn't know what a fossil looked like.
- A squid is sort of like a small jellyfish, except that it has ten to twelve testicles that hang down from its body.
- Water is composed of two gins, oxygin and hydrogin. Oxygin is pure gin. Hydrogin is gin and water.
- Sir Isaac Newton invented the law of gravity, which says no fair jumping up without coming back down.
- Genetics explains why you look like your father and if you don't, why you should.
- Artificial insemination is when the farmer does it to the cow and not the bull.

A Pleasury of
Bloopers

The West Virginia legislature passed a law forbidding "picking flora and fauna within a hundred yards of a highway."

Politicians Incorrect

Many mean things have been said about politicians. They have even been skewered by a fanciful etymology for the word *politics*: *poly*, as in *polygon*, *polygamy*, *polyglot*, and *polytheistic*, means "many"—and *tics*, well, tics are blood-sucking parasites!

Politicians have been riddled by riddles. What's a politician? A man who will double-cross that bridge when he comes to it. How can you tell when a politician is lying? His lips are moving. How are politicians like diapers? They both need to be changed frequently—and for the same reason. What's the difference between a centaur and a senator? One is half man and half horse's ass—and the other is a creature in mythology.

And they have been ridiculed in longer stories:

One day a cannibal took a trip to a neighboring island of cannibals. On the menu of those man-eaters people cost $2 but politicians cost $25.

The visiting cannibal asked, "How come politicians are so expensive?"

The chief answered, "Do you know how hard it is to clean one of those?"

An older couple had a son who was still living at home. The parents were a little worried, as the son was still unable to decide about his future career. They decided to do a small test. They took a $20 bill, a Bible, and a bottle of whiskey, put them on the front hall table, and hid, pretending they were not home.

The father's plan was "If our son takes the money, he will be a businessman. If he takes the Bible, he will be a priest. But if he takes the bottle of whiskey, I'm afraid our son will be a drunkard."

So, the parents waited nervously, hiding in the nearby closet. Peeping through the keyhole, they saw their son arrive. He took the $20 bill, looked at it against the light, and slid it in his pocket. After that, he took the Bible, flicked through it, and kept it. Then, he grabbed the bottle, opened it, and took a sniff, to be assured of the quality. Then he left for his room, carrying all three items.

The father slapped his forehead, and said, "Darn. Our son is going to be a politician!"

Pianist and comedian Victor Borge has observed that "laughter is the shortest distance between two people." I would add that bloopers are the shortest route to laughter and that political bloopers, which are so very public, travel the shortest distance of all.

New York governor Al Smith once gave an address at Sing Sing prison. "My fellow citizens . . ." he began, but suddenly remembered that convicts aren't citizens. He then corrected himself, saying, "My fellow convicts . . ." but he realized that wasn't right either. "Well, anyhow," he said, trying to regain his composure, "I'm glad to see so many of you here."

The vice presidency appears to be an office that scrambles the brain and tangles the tongue. In a televised statement, Vice President Hubert H. Humphrey stated, "No sane person in the country likes the war in Vietnam, and neither does President Johnson." Vice President George Bush explained his secret of teamwork: "For seven and a half years I've worked alongside President Reagan. We've had triumphs. Made some mistakes. We've had some sex . . . uh . . . setbacks."

Second banana Dan Quayle's tongue tangles were so numerous that they spawned an actual periodical that anthologized his Quaylisms. He became unintentionally famous for the likes of:

• We're going to have the best-educated American people in the world.
• We understand the importance of bondage between a mother and child.
• I support efforts to limit the terms of members of Congress, especially members of the House and Senate.
• One word sums up probably the responsibility of any vice president, and that one word is "to be prepared."

A political blooper snooper could fill an entire chapter of a book with the wit and wisdom of Boston mayor Thomas M. Menino, who, on his appointment as acting mayor, announced he was embarking on a period of "transmission." Here are some of the messages he's transmitted:

• The principals deserve the right to install mental detectors in their schools.
• Former mayor John Collins was a man of great, great statue in our city.
• The city shortage of parking spaces is an Alcatraz around my neck.

"And now will y'all stand and be recognized?" asked Texas house speaker Gib Lewis of a group of people in wheelchairs. Lewis became legendary for his monumental twists of the tongue:

• This is unparalyzed in the state's history.
• I want to thank each and every one of you for having extinguished yourselves this session.
• We'll run it up the flagpole and see who salutes that booger.
• There's a lot of uncertainty that's unclear in my mind.

Ambrose Bierce sardonically defined politics as "a strife of interests masquerading as a contest of principles." Napoleon Bonaparte observed, "In politics, an absurdity is not a handicap." Robert Louis Stevenson noted that "politics is perhaps the only profession for which no preparation is thought necessary." And Peter DeVries defined a politician as "a man who can be verbose in fewer words than anyone else." Here are even more political tickles that issued from the golden throats and silver tongues of our appointed and anointed representatives:

l I was under medication when I made the decision not to burn the tapes.

—President Richard Nixon

l This is a great day for France!
—President Richard Nixon, while attending
French president Charles de Gaulle's funeral

l I have opinions of my own—strong opinions—but I don't always agree with them.

—George Bush I

• I have learned from the mistakes I may or may not have made. When I was young and irresponsible, I was young and irresponsible.

—George Bush II

• That depends on what the definition of *is*, is.
—President Bill Clinton, during his deposition
in the Monica Lewinsky case

• I'm not going to have some reporters pawing through our papers. We are the president.

—Hillary Rodham Clinton, commenting on
the release of subpoenaed documents

• The president has kept all the promises he intended to keep.
—Clinton aide George Stephanopolous

- I didn't accept it. I received it.

> —*Richard Allen, national security adviser to President Reagan,*
> *explaining the $1,000 cash and two watches he was given*
> *by two Japanese journalists after he helped arrange a*
> *private interview for them with First Lady Nancy Reagan*

- The West Virginia legislature passed a law forbidding "picking flora and fauna within a hundred yards of a highway."
- Capital punishment is our society's recognition of the sanctity of human life.

> —*Utah senator Orrin Hatch, explaining his support of the death penalty*

- Statistics show that teen pregnancy drops off significantly after age 25.

> —*Mary Ann Tebedo, Colorado state representative*

- I am privileged to speak at this millstone in the history of this college.

> —*New Hampshire governor John King at a*
> *Dartmouth College graduation*

- I wanted all my ducks in a row, so if we did get into a posture, we could pretty much slam-dunk this thing and put it to bed.

> —*Lee Cooke, mayor of Austin, Texas*

- If you've seen one redwood tree, you've seen them all.

> —*forestry expert Ronald Reagan*

- Facts are stupid things.

> —*Ronald Reagan, misquoting John Adams in*
> *a speech to the 1984 Republican convention*

- The Internet is a great way to get on the net.

> —*presidential candidate Bob Dole*

- Things are more like they are now than they ever were before.

  —*President Dwight Eisenhower*

- I want to make sure everybody who has a job wants a job.

  —*President George Bush*

- He didn't say that. He was reading what was given to him in a speech.

  —*Richard Darman, director of OMB, explaining why President Bush wasn't following up on his campaign pledge that there would be no loss of wetlands*

- There are still places where people think the function of the media is to provide information.

  —*Dan Rottenberg, White House spokesperson*

- I'm not against the blacks, and a lot of the good blacks will attest to that.

  —*Arizona governor Evan Mecham*

- What he does on his own time is up to him.

  —*Harlon Copeland, Sheriff of Bexar County, Texas, when one of his deputies was caught exposing himself to a child*

- I don't know anyone here that's been killed by a handgun.

  —*Louisiana representative Avery Alexander*

- I can't believe that we are going to let a majority of people decide what's best for this state.

  —*Louisiana representative John Travis*

- We don't want to open a box of Pandoras.

  —*New Mexico governor Bruce King*

- The exports include thumbscrews and cattle prods, just routine items for the police.
> —U.S. Commerce Department spokesman, on a regulation
> allowing the export of various products abroad

- What is the state of North Carolina going to do about its bludgeoning prison population?
> —Iowa state senator Maggie Tinsman

- Senator Harper has been introducing amendments up the kazoo for the last 24 hours, but this is really one you ought to look at.
> —Iowa state senator Mary Neuhauser

- If English was good enough for Jesus Christ, then it's good enough for me.
> —an Arkansas congressman to the
> Joint National Committee on Language

A habitually cautious U.S. congressman had several too many at a luncheon party. Near the end of the meal, he rose to make a few remarks. So carried away was he by his eloquence that before he wound up, he declared himself on a half dozen key questions being debated in the House at the time.

When he sat down, several colleagues marched over to congratulate him, one going as far as to say, "Brother, you sure gave it to them today. You showed with crystal clarity where you stood on all those controversial issues plaguing this body."

The congressman turned deathly pale. "Good God," he gulped. "I DID?"

"The defecation of character must cease," once roared James McSheehy, of the San Francisco Board of Supervisors. And the character of this defecation by politicians must also cease one day, we hope. The legendary speaker of the House, Tip O'Neil, once proclaimed that "all politics is local." In the light of the political swill spewing around the media, he might have said, "All politics is loco."

THE POLY-TICKLE HALL OF FAME

- The police are not here to create disorder! They are here to preserve disorder!

    —*Chicago mayor Richard J. Daley*

- If Lincoln were alive today, he'd roll over in his grave.

    —*President Gerald Ford*

- I wish the Arabs and the Jews would settle their differences like Christian gentlemen.

    —*attributed to Arthur Balfour and others*

- The streets are safe in Philadelphia. It's the people who make them unsafe.

    —*Philadelphia mayor Frank Rizzo*

- On the manhood thing, I'll put mine up against his any time!

    —*President George Bush, responding to accusations by*
    Walter Mondale in a vice-presidential debate

*José Canseco's agent says that José wants to play
the outfield in the worst way.*

Sore Sport

Steve Spurrier, Florida football coach, once informed Gator fans that a fire at Auburn's football dormitory had destroyed 20 books. "But the real tragedy," Spurrier explained, "was that 15 hadn't been colored yet."

Shelby Metcalf, basketball coach at Texas A&M, recounted what he told a player who received four F's and one D: "Son, looks to me like you're spending too much time on one subject."

These barbs are tossed with tongue firmly planted in cheek, but you have to wonder about the brain power of our nation's athletes. As a senior basketball player at the University of Pittsburgh noted sagely, "I'm going to graduate on time, no matter how long it takes."

- It would permanently hurt a batter for a long time.

  —Pete Rose, baseball's all-time hit champion,
  on the effect of a brushback pitch

- It's about 90 percent strength and 40 percent technique.

  —Johnny Walker, world middle-weight wrist-wrestling champion,
  on what it takes to be great

- We're going to turn this team around 360 degrees.

  —Jason Kidd, on being drafted by the Dallas Mavericks

- When I get too much rest, I'm usually erotic.

  —New York Yankees pitching ace Roger Clemens

- On what?

  —Chris Eubank, when an interviewer asked him,
  "Have you thought about writing your autobiography?"

- We have only one person to blame, and that's each other.

  —New York Ranger Barry Beck, who started a brawl during a
  Stanley Cup playoff game, for which his team was penalized

- All I said was that the trades were stupid and dumb, and they took that and blew it all out of proportion.

  —Ron Davis, Minnesota Twins pitcher, commenting on press reports that
  he had criticized team management for trading away top players

- Me and George and Billy are two of a kind.

  —Mickey Rivers, on his warm relationship with Yankee owner
  George Steinbrenner and manager Billy Martin

- You mean now?

  —Legendary Yankees catcher Yogi Berra, when asked what time it was

- Whatever is going to happen is going to happen when it happens, regardless of what happens.

  —baseball player Mike LaValliere

- He treats us like men. He lets us wear earrings.
  —Torrin Polk, University of Houston receiver,
  on his coach, John Jenkins

- My sister's expecting a baby, and I don't know if I'm going to be an uncle or an aunt.
  —Chuck Nevitt, North Carolina State basketball player,
  explaining to his coach why he appeared nervous at practice

- I think that the team that wins game five will win the series—unless we lose game five.
  —Charles Barkley, star forward for the Houston Rockets,
  predicting the outcome of the playoffs

- I can shoot with my left hand, and I can shoot with my right hand. Damn, I must be amphibious.
  —Charles Shackleford, North Carolina State basketball player,
  explaining to reporters his ability to drive to the basket

- If I had not lost, I would have won.
  —tennis star Serena Williams, after failing
  to win the French Open

- Where's the football field?
  —tennis star Jennifer Capriati, while being shown
  Notre Dame cathedral in Paris

- Yes, we'll be able to hang our heads high in the off-season.
  —quarterback Warren Moon, after leading the AFC
  to a Pro Bowl victory

- That's so when I forget how to spell my name, I can still find my #%@# clothes.
  —Stu Grimson, Chicago Blackhawks left wing, explaining why he
  keeps a color photo of himself above his locker

• I don't remember what happened in the Davis Cup, although I do remember.

—*Russian tennis star Yevgeny Kafelnikov*

• We've got our backs to the driver's seat.
—*Denver Broncos halfback Otis Armstrong, on his team's future*

• I want all the kids to do what I do, to look up to me. I want all kids to copulate me.

—*Chicago Clubs outfielder Andre Dawson*

• I want to rush for 1,000 or 1,500 yards, whichever comes first.
—*New Orleans Saints running back George Rogers,*
when asked about the upcoming season

• I can't really remember the names of the clubs that we went to.
—*Shaquille O'Neal, star center for the Los Angeles Lakers, on*
whether he had visited the Parthenon during his visit to Greece

• Definitely. I mean I'm not so arrogant that I can't forgive.
—*New York Knicks forward Latrell Sprewell when asked if he would*
consider meeting with his former coach, P. J. Carlesimo,
whom he had tried to strangle two years earlier

• Detroit Piston center Reggie Harding donned a stocking mask and robbed at gunpoint a liquor store he frequented. When the store manager asked him, "What are you doing, Reggie?" Harding replied, "It ain't me, man!"

• Let's not bash just the players. Dallas Cowboys coaching legend Tom Landry once observed, "Football is an incredible game. Sometimes it's so incredible, it's unbelievable." Incredible are the pronouncements of Pittsburgh Steelers coach Bill Cowher. Besides being one of the most fiery coaches in the National Football League, Cowher is a master of the malaprop:

- There are some teams who will try to circumcise the rules.
- It's a no-win, no-lose situation.
- He came of age and surpassed it.
—*on quarterback Kordell Stewart's performance in a comeback victory*

Cowher's immortal phraseology ranks high among the athletic whiz and witdom of owners, coaches, managers, and trainers. These luminaries apparently throw as many screwballs, airballs, and interceptions as those whom they own, coach, manage, and train:

- David Cone is in a class by himself with only three or four other players.
   —*Yankees owner George Steinbrenner, evaluating his ace pitcher*

- Sometimes, even if you spend lots of money on a baseball team, it won't win. Things happen. Injuries. Guys fall down. One of your pitchers can get one of those rotary cuffs.
   —*Ted Turner, Atlanta Braves owner*

- I'm not allowed to comment on lousy officiating.
   —*Jim Finks, New Orleans Saints general manager, when asked after a loss what he thought of the referees*

- Even Napoleon had his Watergate.
   —*Danny Ozark, Philadelphia Phillies manager, commenting on a ten-game losing streak*

- When it rains, it snows.
   —*Florida football coach Bobby Bowden, on learning that one of his players had had another brush with the law*

- It's the kind of book that you can never pick up once you put it down.
   —*Pat Williams, Philadelphia 76ers general manager, on Charles Barkley's autobiography*

- She was a super filly, a Christian, and a good friend.

    —trainer Henry Cecil on the retirement of his horse Borsa Sham

- How do you figure this game? You really can't. Just when you think you have, someone throws you a great curveball, and there you are walking back to the dugout with your head between your legs.

    —baseball coach Davey Lopes

- In the legendary name of the greatest hockey player in history—what's his name? . . .

    —hockey expert Don King

- If we're gonna win, we have to play up to and beyond our potential. We're capable of doing that.

    —Dallas Mavericks coach Don Nelson

- That was the nail that got the coffin going.

    —Bob Toledo, UCLA football coach, on an interception against his team in the Rose Bowl

- He's a guy who gets up at six o'clock in the morning regardless of what time it is.

    —Lou Duva, veteran boxing trainer, on the spartan training regime of heavyweight Andrew Golota

Washington Redskins quarterback-turned-announcer Joe Theismann once commented on the penchant of football commentators like him to label coaches "geniuses": "Nobody in football should be called a genius. A genius is a guy like Norman Einstein."

Well, Joe, you are indeed no Einstein, and neither are your colleagues in the broadcast booth. A Kansas City announcer exulted, "Incredible is too conservative an adjective to describe this team. They are unbelievable." Some of the drivel that dribbles from the silvertongues in the broadcast booth is indeed so incredible that it's unbelievable:

- We started with 53,000 people. Half are gone, but, surprisingly, most are still here!

    —Jerry Coleman, in the 13th inning of a 16-inning game

• Oh, that Lankford and McGee, the trio of 'em. They're a one-man wrecking crew.
—*Mike Shannon, announcing a St. Louis Cardinals baseball game*

• I think players and caddies have to have good intercourse on a week like this.
—*Mary Bryan, ESPN golf announcer, during the Rochester International*

• Histrionics are against him.
—*John Tesh, commenting on a gymnast's chances for an Olympic medal*

• He fakes a bluff.
—*Ron Fairley, New York Giants announcer*

• Fans, don't fail to miss tomorrow's game.
—*Dizzy Dean, baseball great turned announcer*

• Statistically, when the Hawks score more than 100 points and the defense holds the other team to less than 100, they almost always win.
—*Atlanta Hawks announcer during a game. (This is the same kind of logic that reposes in a University of Maryland news release: "Maryland is 15-0, undefeated, when it outscores its opponents.")*

• He is the only ambidextrous kicker in the NFL.
—*San Diego Chargers announcer*

• The Utah Jazz know where their butt is breaded.
—*basketball announcer Quinn Buckner*

• Andre Vandapole has four silver medals in cyclocross, and none of them gold.
—*Phil Liggott*

• Right after hurling his perfect game in the 1956 World Series, Don Larson was asked by a reporter, "Was that the best game you've ever pitched?"

• This run of 24 games without defeat must be like a millstone on your shoulders.

• José Canseco's agent says that José wants to play the outfield in the worst way.

THE SPORTSCASTING HALL OF FAME

- It appears as though the Achilles' heel of the Eagles' defense is about to rear its ugly head.
- There's a long drive! Winfield is going back, back, back! He hits his head against the wall! It's rolling into second base!
- Arnie Palmer, usually a great putter, seems to be having trouble with his long putts. However, he has no trouble dropping his shorts.
- He threw 100 pitches in six innings, and that's a mouthful.
- He's already got two championship rings under his belt.

"What were all the grown-ups doing?"

Kidding Around in Church

Bill Keane, creator of *The Family Circus* cartoon strip, tells of a time when he was penciling one of his cartoons and his son Jeffy said, "Daddy, how do you know what to draw?"

Keane explained, "God tells me."

At which point Jeffy asked, "Then why do you keep erasing parts of it?"

There are times when parents wish that the innocent comments from their children could be erased. "To err is human, to forgive divine," wrote the poet Alexander Pope. I say, "To forgive is human, to err, divine." And some of the most divine bloopers drop from the mouths of our innocent young as wholly holy bloopers:

- A boy was watching his father, a pastor, write a sermon. "How do you know what to say?" he asked.

"Why, God tells me."

"Oh," asked the boy. "Then why do you keep crossing things out?"

- Two daughters had been given parts in a Christmas pageant at their church. At dinner that night, they got into an argument as to who had the more important role. Finally the ten-year-old said to her younger sister, "Well, you just ask Mom. She'll tell you it's much harder to be a virgin than it is to be an angel."

- One Sunday morning, the pastor noticed little Barry was staring up at the large plaque that hung in the foyer of the church. It was covered with names, and small American flags were mounted on either side of it. The seven-year-old had been staring at the plaque for some time, so the pastor walked up, stood beside the boy, and said quietly, "Good morning, Barry."

"Good morning, Pastor," replied the young man, still focused on the plaque. "Pastor McGhee, what is this?" Barry asked.

"Well, son, it's a memorial to all the young men and women who died in the service."

Soberly, they stood together, staring at the large plaque. Little Barry's voice was barely audible when he asked, "Which one, the 9:00 or the 10:30 service?"

- A little boy walked down the aisle at a wedding. As he made his way to the front, he would take two steps, stop, and turn to the crowd, alternating between the bride's side and the groom's side. While facing the crowd, he would put his hands up like claws and roar—and so it went, step, step, ROAR, step, step, ROAR, all the way down the aisle.

As you can imagine, the crowd was near tears from laughing so hard by the time he reached the pulpit. The little boy, however, was getting more and more distressed from all the laughing, and was also near tears by the time he reached the pulpit.

When asked what he was doing, the child sniffed back his tears and said, "I was being the Ring Bear."

- At the Henry Street Hebrew School, Mr. Goldblatt, the new

teacher, finished the day's lesson. It was now time for the usual question period.

"Mr. Goldblatt," announced little Joey, "there's something I can't figure out."

"What's that, Joey?" asked the teacher.

"Well, according to the Bible, the Children of Israel crossed the Red Sea, right?"

"Right."

"And the Children of Israel beat up the Philistines, right?"

"Er, right."

"And the Children of Israel built the Temple, right?"

"Again you're right."

"And the Children of Israel fought the Egyptians, and the Children of Israel fought the Romans, and the Children of Israel wuz always doing somethin' important, right?"

"All that is right, too," agreed Mr. Goldblatt. "So what's your question?"

"What I want to know is this," demanded Joey. "What were all the grown-ups doing?"

• A Sunday school teacher was discussing the Ten Commandments with her five- and six-year-olds. After explaining the commandment to "honor thy father and thy mother," she asked, "Is there a commandment that teaches us how to treat our brothers and sisters?" Without missing a beat, one little boy, the oldest in his family, answered, "Thou shall not kill."

• A Sunday school student was asked to list the Ten Commandments in any order. His answer was "3, 6, 1, 8, 4, 5, 9, 2, 10, 7."

• After the church service, a little boy told the pastor, "When I grow up, I'm going to give you some money."

"Well, thank you," the pastor replied, "but why?"

"Because my daddy says you're one of the poorest preachers we've ever had."

• A couple invited some people to dinner. At the table, the mother turned to her six-year-old daughter and said, "Would you like to say the blessing?"

"I wouldn't know what to say," she replied.

"Just say what you hear Mommy say," Mother said.

The little girl bowed her head and said, "Dear Lord, why on earth did I invite all these people to dinner?"

• A mother took her three-year-old daughter to church for the first time. The church lights were lowered, and then the choir came down the aisle, carrying lighted candles. All was quiet until the little one started to sing in a loud voice, "Happy Birthday to you. . . ."

• At the beginning of a children's sermon, one girl came up to the altar wearing a beautiful dress. As the children sat down around the pastor, the pastor leaned over and said to the girl, "That is a very pretty dress. Is it your Easter dress?"

The girl replied almost directly into the pastor's clip-on microphone, "Yes, and my mom says it's a bitch to iron."

• A Sunday school teacher asked her class, "Does anyone here know what we mean by sins of omission?"

One of the girls replied, "Aren't those the sins that we should have committed, but didn't?"

• Six-year-old Angie and her four-year-old brother Joel were sitting together in church. Joel giggled, sang, and talked out loud. Finally, his big sister had enough.

"You're not supposed to talk out loud in church."

"Why? Who's going to stop me?" Joel asked.

Angie pointed to the back of the church and said, "See those two men standing by the door? They're hushers."

• When, during the service, the priest intoned, "The peace of the Lord be with you," a three-year-old girl responded, "And pizza with you."

• During a children's sermon, the priest asked the children what "amen" means. A little boy raised his hand and said, "It means 'Tha-tha-tha-that's all folks!'"

• A ten-year-old, under the tutelage of her grandmother, became quite knowledgeable about the Bible. Then one day she floored her grandmother by asking, "Whose virgin was the mother of Jesus: the Virgin Mary or the King James Virgin?"

• A Sunday school class was studying the Ten Commandments. On that day, the discussion concerned the Tenth Commandment. The teacher asked if anyone could tell what it was that the Tenth Commandment forbade. Sally raised her hand, stood tall, and quoted, "Thou shalt not cover thy neighbor's wife."

• A Sunday school teacher asked her class why Joseph and Mary took Jesus with them to Jerusalem. A young girl answered, "Because they couldn't get a baby-sitter."

• Another Sunday school teacher was instructing her class. Just before she dismissed them to go to church, she asked them, "Why it is necessary to be quiet in church?"

Little Gilbert was quick to blurt out what he was certain was the correct answer: "Because people are sleeping!"

• Maud, age six, said to her parents, "I'm going up to bed now. When I say my prayers, do either of you want anything?"

• As the class was discussing the nativity, a first-grader in Sunday school said that after Jesus was born, Mary wrapped him in toddler clothes.

• A four-year-old girl was learning to recite the Lord's Prayer all by herself without help from her mother. She concluded her recitation with the line "and lead us not into temptation, but deliver us some e-mail. Amen."

Amen!

THE SUNDAY SCHOOL BLOOPERS HALL OF FAME

- Lot's wife was a pillar of salt by day and a ball of fire by night.
- Moses went up on Mount Cyanide to get the Ten Commandments, but he died before he ever reached Canada.
- Solomon had 300 wives and 500 porcupines.
- Jesus was born because Mary had an immaculate contraption.
- An epistle is the wife of an apostle.

The music for today's service was all composed by George Frideric Handel in celebration of the 300th anniversary of his birth.

Parish the Thought

The Bible tells us that "a cheerful heart is good medicine, but a crushed spirit dries up the bones." (Proverbs 17:22.) Certain church bulletins and orders of service cheer the heart and uplift the spirit, even though the good people who write the texts for those bulletins and speak the speeches in those sanctuaries aren't always aware of the effects of their prose.

Over the massive front doors of a church, these words were inscribed: "The Gate of Heaven." Below that was a small cardboard sign that read, "Please use other entrance."

On another church door was posted the message "This is the gate of

Heaven. Enter ye all by this door." Below it was taped a smaller sign: "This door is kept locked because of the draft. Please use side entrance."

Another church advertised:

```
┌─────────────────────────────────────┐
│                                     │
│              BINGO!                 │
│       IMMACULATE CONCEPTION         │
│         TONIGHT AT 7 P.M.           │
│                                     │
└─────────────────────────────────────┘
```

In front of another church appeared a sign that advertised, "Millions long for immorality and don't know what to do on a rainy day."

Outside of yet another church a sign proclaimed, "Lenten Worship Sermon: The Surest Road to Hell." Below that reposed the instructions "Transportation Available. Please call before noon Saturday."

And how inviting would you find a church that advertised, "This is the First Baptist Church where you are welcome"?

Enter church, all ye blooper lovers, and witness the unholy errors that make some churches more fun to attend than others:

• The Ladies Bible Study will be held Thursday morning at 10. All ladies are invited to lunch in the Fellowship Hall after the B.S. is done.

• The peacemaking meeting scheduled for today has been canceled due to a conflict.

• Men's prayer breakfast. No charge, but your damnation will be gratefully accepted.

• Missionary from Africa speaking at Calvary Memorial Church in Racine. Name: Bertha Belch. Announcement: "Come tonight and hear Bertha Belch all the way from Africa."

• Would the congregation please note that the bowl at the back of the church labeled "For the Sick" is for monetary donations only.

• Barbara Chisolm remains in the hospital and needs blood donors for more transfusions. She is also having trouble sleeping and requests tapes of Pastor Jack's sermons.

• The cost for attending the Prayer & Fasting conference includes meals.

- Lecture Tuesday evening at 7:00 on "The Christian and Sexuality." The pubic is invited.
- At the Women's Fellowship, the ladies showed off their knitting and crotches.
- The church is glad to have with us today as our guest minister the Reverend Raymond Green, who has Mrs. Green with him. After the service, we request that all remain in the sanctuary for the Hanging of the Greens.
- Want to make a little extra money? Christian church in Mantua is in market for a choir director. If you are interested, call 555-5555/leave mess.
- Visit our Christian bookstore, where Jesus is King and carries every translation of the Holy Bible.
- The 1991 Spring Council retreat will be hell May 10 & 11.
- The third verse of "Blessed Assurance" will be sung without musical accomplishment.
- Couples should contact the pastor at least six months in advance of marriage, even if a firm hate has been established.
- The Over 60s Choir will be disbanded for the summer with the thanks of the entire church.
- Pastor is on vacation. Massages can be given to church secretary.
- The associate minister unveiled the church's new tithing campaign slogan last Sunday: "I Upped My Pledge—Now Up Yours."
- Eight new choir robes are currently needed, due to the addition of new members and to the deterioration of some older ones.
- Scouts are saving aluminum cans, bottles, and other items to be recycled. Proceeds will go to cripple children.
- Our choir sang in a broadcast from Minneapolis. It was nice to hear them and realize they were nearly a thousand miles away.
- At the annual all-women's church party, Mrs. Dixon will give the medication.
- A new loudspeaker system has been installed in the church. It was given by one of our members in honor of his wife.
- The senior choir invites any member of the congregation who enjoys sinning to join the choir.
- During the Burning Bowel Service you are given the opportunity to let go and release anything unwanted in your life.

- The music for today's service was all composed by George Frideric Handel in celebration of the 300th anniversary of his birth.
- Hymn: "Wise Up, O Men of God"
- The next hymn will be "Angels We Have Heard Get High."
- Postlude: "Rejoice Ye Pure in Heat."
- Next Thursday, there will be tryouts for the choir. They need all the help they can get.
- It would be a great help towards keeping the churchyard in good order if others would follow the example of others who clip the grass on their own graves.
- Remember in prayer the many who are sick of our church and community.
- This morning's sermon: "Jesus Walks on the Water." Tonight's sermon: "Searching for Jesus."
- Thursday night—Potluck Supper. Prayer and medication to follow.
- Mr. Peabody was elected and has accepted the position of church warden. We could not get a better man.
- Please join us as we show our support for Amy and Alan, who are preparing for the girth of their first child.
- The Lutheran Men's Group will meet at 6 P.M. Steak, mashed potatoes, green beans, bread, and dessert will be served for a nominal feel.
- Again this year St. Gertrude's will roll out the red carpet for our archdiocese seminarians and show them our famous hospitality. If you would like to hose one (or two) of the men for the weekend in your home, please call the parish office and leave your name.
- Reverend H. J. Dick, pastor of Emmaus Mennonite Church near Whitewater, Kansas, came to the end of a very heavy day at the New Year's Eve midnight service. Getting his tongue tangled, he announced, "Let us now stand and sing 'Another Dear Is Yawning.'"
- Next Sunday is the family hayride and bonfire at the Taylors'. Bring your own hot dogs and guns. Bring a friend.
- Please keep a close watch on your children as they play outside. Several snakes have been seen around the edge of the woods. Our Easter egg hunt will take place this Saturday here at the church.
- In the future, ushers will swat latecomers to the service.
- Ushers will eat latecomers.

THE CHURCH BULLETIN
HALL OF FAME

- The ladies of the church have cast off clothing of every kind, and these can be seen in the church basement Friday afternoon.
- This being Easter Sunday, we will ask Mrs. White to come forward to lay an egg on the altar.
- This afternoon, there will be a meeting in the south and north end of the church. Children will be baptized at both ends.
- Tomorrow's lecture will be "Recycling—Our Garbage Is a Resource." There will be a potluck supper at 6 P.M.
- Support our church rummage sale: a good opportunity to get rid of anything not worth keeping but too good to throw away. Bring your husband.

Q. Did you see him bite off the plaintiff's ear?
A. Nope, Your Honor, but I did see him spit it out.

Court Comedians

The media frequently portray the courtroom drama of penetrating interrogation, tight-lipped testimony, and riveting revelations. But the media usually overlook the courtly humor of loopy logic, bubble-off-plumb vocabulary, and questions that ought to be taken out and shot. Fortunately, an army of certified court reporters take down verbatim transcripts that preserve the gavel-to-gabble humor.

Each of the vignettes that follow actually took place in the law-and-disorder atmosphere of a real courtroom. They come to us courtesy of court reporters around the nation, America's keepers of the word. Nobody appreciates a good chuckle more than court reporters. In fact, their lively sense of humor may be essential for longevity in the field. Not insensitive to the gravity of legal strife, reporters recognize hilarity in the rough-and-bumble exchanges that transpire in our halls of justice. Such a sense of humor relieves the tension, dispels the gloom of the often-dark content, and provides much-needed comic relief.

A defense attorney was cross-examining a police officer during a felony trial. It went like this:

Q. Officer, did you see my client fleeing the scene?

A. No, sir, but I subsequently observed a person matching the description of the offender running several blocks away.

Q. Officer, who provided this description?

A. The officer who responded to the scene.

Q. A fellow officer provided the description of this so-called offender. Do you trust your fellow officers?

A. Yes, sir, with my life.

Q. With your life? Let me ask you this then, officer. Do you have a locker room in the police station—a room where you change your clothes in preparation for your daily duties?

A. Yes, sir, we do.

Q. And do you have a locker in that room?

A. Yes, sir, I do.

Q. And do you have a lock on your locker?

A. Yes, sir.

Q. Now why is it, officer, if you trust your fellow officers with your life, that you find it necessary to lock your locker in a room you share with those same officers?

A. You see, sir, we share the building with a court complex, and sometimes lawyers have been known to walk through that room.

With that, the courtroom erupted in laughter and a prompt recess was called.

Hear ye! Hear ye! Court is now in session!:

Q. Now it's a fact, isn't it, that whenever your husband leaves town on his job as an over-the-road truck driver, another man comes to live in your house?

A. That's a lie! My husband is not an over-the-road truck driver!

Q. Have you changed your mind about your dissolution of marriage?
A. No, I'm still disillusioned.

◎

Q. Please describe the woman.
A. This young lady walked very close to me, and it was obvious that underneath her clothing she wore nothing.

◎

Q. Did the perpetrator have facial hair?
A. Yes. Eyebrows.

◎

Q. Did you see him bite off the plaintiff's ear?
A. Nope, Your Honor, but I did see him spit it out.

◎

Q. Have you ever been accused of taking anything from your employer that you were not entitled to, Mrs. Sanders?
A. Do you mean other than my paycheck?

◎

THE COURT: Sir, I have an undated letter in the file purportedly signed by you stating why you missed your court date. Is this your letter, and is this your signature, sir?
A. Yes, Your Honor.
THE COURT: The letter states you missed your last court date because your aunt was in the hospital dying of prostate cancer.
A. That's right, and she's still in there, too.
THE COURT: Sir, your aunt doesn't have a prostate.
A. Oh.

◎

THE COURT: How old are you?
A. Seventeen, and I've been masturbated.

THE COURT: What is it exactly, sir, that you are trying to tell me?

A. Me and my folks went to the courthouse last week, signed the forms. I'm on my own now.

THE COURT: Are you trying to tell me you are emancipated?

A. That's it; that's the word.

◎

Q. Miss, were you cited in the accident?

A. Yes sir, I was so 'cited I peed all over myself.

◎

Q. What gear were you in at the moment of the impact?

A. Gucci sweats and Reeboks.

◎

Q. You say my client had sex with you?

A. Uh-huh.

Q. Tell the jury, is my client circumcised or uncircumcised.

A. I don't know him that well. I don't think he even goes to church.

◎

Q. Did you blow your horn or anything?

A. After the accident?

Q. Before the accident.

A. Sure, I played for ten years. I even went to school for it.

◎

Q. Do you know if your daughter has ever been involved in the voodoo occult?

A. We both do.

Q. Voodoo?

A. We do.

Q. You do?

A. Yes, voodoo.

◎

Q. And this card contains a print of each finger of Mr. McGinty's hands; is that correct?

A. It's all five fingers of the right hand, all five fingers of the left hand, plus all four fingers and the thumbs.

◎

Q. And what is your brother's name?

A. Gerald Gassa, the same name as my last name, but his first is Gerald.

Q. How old is Gerald?

A. He's a year younger than me.

Q. And how old are you?

A. I'm a year older than him.

◎

Q. How far apart are the rungs on the ladder?

A. They're usually about 12 inches to a foot.

◎

Q. Mr. Gonzales, where do you live?

A. Mexia, Texas.

Q. Have you lived in Mexia all your life?

A. Not yet.

◎

Q. Ma'am, you say your husband beat you?

A. Yes. I even went to the hospital.

Q. Well, did you ever give him provocation?

A. (tearfully) He could have had it any time he wanted!

◎

Q. The truth of the matter is that you were not an unbiased, objective witness, isn't it? You too were shot in the whole ordeal?

A. No, sir. I was shot midway between the ordeal and the navel.

◎

Q. Are you qualified to give a urine sample?

A. Yes, I have been since early childhood.

A Texas attorney, realizing he was on the verge of unleashing a stupid question, interrupted himself and said, "Your Honor, I'd like to strike the next question." Unfortunately, other attorneys have failed to interrupt themselves, as witness this exchange:

LAWYER: You signed the death certificate?
PATHOLOGIST: Yes.
Q. Before you signed the certificate, did you take his pulse?
A. No.
Q. Did you check to see if he was breathing?
A. No.
Q. Did you listen for his heartbeat?
A. No.
Q. Well, how could you be sure he was dead?
A. I've got his brain in a jar on my desk, but I guess he could be walking around practicing law somewhere.

It appears that a number of attorneys are walking around with their brains in jars. Here's a Witless Sampler of the kinds of questions lawyers ask when they run their mouths full spigot:

- How long have you been a French Canadian?
- Were you present in court this morning when you were sworn in?
- So you were gone until you returned?
- The youngest son, the 20-year-old, how old is he?
- Was it you or your younger brother who was killed in the war?
- Now doctor, isn't it true that when a person dies in his sleep, he doesn't know about it until the next morning?

Q. She had three children, right?
A. Yes.
Q. How many were boys?
A. None.
Q. Were there any girls?

⊚

Q. Was the defendant like a son to you?

A. Yes.

Q. And was he like a daughter to your wife?

◎

Q. Did you leave a note on the other car that you had been the one who damaged his car?

A. Yes.

Q. Do you still have that note?

◎

Q. Mr. Sullivan, you went on a rather elaborate honeymoon, didn't you?

A. I went to Europe, sir.

Q. And you took your new wife?

◎

Q. Now, when the officer told you if you were indignant, the court would appoint you an attorney, did you know what he meant by that, by indignant?

A. Yeah. It means I ain't got no money.

◎

Q. How many years have you been a polygamist?

A. Well, I have only one wife, but I have been a polygraphist for 20 years.

◎

Q. You know he died in May of 1994?

A. Well, I knew he died in 1994.

Q. So you met him just before he died for the first time?

◎

Q. Do you have any sort of medical disability?

A. Legally blind.

Q. Does that create substantial problems with your eyesight as far as seeing things?

THE PRE-TRIAL HALL OF FAME

Disorder in the court can begin even before the testimony. A defendant pled, "Your Honor, as God is my judge, I didn't do it! I'm not guilty!"

Replied the judge, "He isn't! I am! You did! You are!"

The hilarity can start even at the swearing-in of a witness:

CLERK: Please repeat after me: I swear by Almighty God.

WITNESS: I swear by Almighty God.

CLERK: That the evidence that I give.

WITNESS: That's right.

CLERK: Repeat it.

WITNESS: Repeat it.

CLERK: No! Repeat what I said.

WITNESS: What you said when?

CLERK: That the evidence that I give.

WITNESS: That the evidence that I give.

CLERK: Shall be the truth and . . .

WITNESS: It will, and nothing but the truth!

CLERK: Please, just repeat after me: Shall be the truth and . . .

WITNESS: I'm not a scholar, you know.

CLERK: We can appreciate that. Just repeat after me: Shall be the truth and . . .

WITNESS: Shall be the truth and . . .

CLERK: Say, "Nothing."

WITNESS: Okay. [Witness remains silent.]

CLERK: No! Don't say nothing. Say, "Nothing but the truth."

WITNESS: Yes.

CLERK: Can't you say, "Nothing but the truth"?

WITNESS: Yes.

CLERK: Well? Do so.

WITNESS: You're confusing me.

CLERK: Just say, "Nothing but the truth."

WITNESS: Is that all?

CLERK: Yes.

WITNESS: Okay. I understand.

CLERK: Then say it.

WITNESS: What?

CLERK: "Nothing but the truth."

WITNESS: But I do! That's just it.

CLERK: You must say, "Nothing but the truth."

WITNESS: I will say, "Nothing but the truth"!

CLERK: Please, just repeat these four words: "Nothing," "But," "The," "Truth."

WITNESS: What? You mean, like, now?

CLERK: Yes! Now. Please. Just say those four words.

WITNESS: "Nothing." "But." "The." "Truth."

CLERK: Thank you.

WITNESS: I'm just not a scholar.

The baby was delivered, the cord clamped and cut and handed to the pediatrician, who breathed and cried immediately.

Transcendental Medication

Do you think that all hospitals and doctors' offices are stages for nail-biting, pulse-quickening drama? Do you envision grim-faced doctors and nurses hovering above the operating table making life-preserving decisions? I hope I'm not ruining anybody's view of our health-care system, but often premedicated comedy can infiltrate America's halls of medicine.

Here, from my friends in the American Association of Medical Transcriptionists, are some real-life doctors' dictations that need a prescription—or perhaps a lawsuit for alienation of infections! Physicians, please try a little harder to cross thy *t*'s and dot thy *i*'s. Physicians, heal thyselves!

- He collapsed on the sidewalk and died without medical assistance.
- He is married but not currently smoking.
- The baby was delivered, the cord clamped and cut and handed to the pediatrician, who breathed and cried immediately.
- He has one actinic keratosis behind his right eye, and he has one on his left ear, and one on his right neck.
- The patient had ear wax impaction, so I removed the ear. It was red and tender afterwards.
- Rectal exam revealed a normal-size thyroid.
- His progress was poor, having a massive cerebral hemorrhoid.
- Bleeding started in the rectal area and continued all the way to Los Angeles.
- He also has noted impotence and an inability to maintain an erection for the past several months. He is requesting assistance in this area.
- There are no elements of dyssomnia or other sleep disturbance, and this young man reports that he is waking refreshed from school.
- The patient had waffles for breakfast and anorexia for lunch.
- She stated that she had been constipated for most of her life until 1989, when she got a divorce.
- When he was diagnosed as a baby, there were only 20 others known in the province.
- The throat shows tonsils that have been removed.
- For the last three weeks his nose has been running pretty much nonstop. It is running down the back of his throat.
- The patient is a 53-year-old police officer who was found unconscious by his bicycle.
- He was in a coma for a lengthy amount of time, receiving massive head injuries and brain damage.
- Her only other complaint on review of systems was of decreased hearing, largely when her teenage children are talking to her.
- The patient is married but sexually active.

- The lab test indicated abnormal lover function.
- Exam of genitalia reveals that he is circus sized.
- Both her old and new noses have been placed in our album.
- The skin was moist and dry.
- Patient was alert and unresponsive.
- Between you and me, we ought to be able to get this lady pregnant.
- The patient was in his usual state of good health until his airplane ran out of gas and crashed.
- I saw your patient today, who is still under our car for physical therapy.
- Examination reveals a well-developed male lying in bed with his family in no distress.
- The patient lives at home with his mother, father, and pet turtle, who is presently enrolled in day care three times a week.
- Both breasts are equal and reactive to light and accommodation.
- She is numb from her toes down.
- I sounded her with a #26 sound, and she let out a scream that broke two beakers in the examining room and caused a patient at the delicatessen around the corner to aspirate his Reuben sandwich.
- Exam of genitalia was completely negative except for the right foot.
- While in the emergency room, she was examined, X-rated, and sent home.
- The patient suffers from occasional, constant, infrequent headaches.
- The patient suffered a fatal demise.
- She will return to me when she wishes to become pregnant.
- Type this list of numbers alphabetically.
- His headaches are precipitated by drinking one beer, but he can avoid them by drinking all night.
- Past history includes puberty and back surgery.
- When you pin him down, he has some slowing of his stream.
- To the best of the patient's knowledge, he has never fathered children, nor has his wife.
- Considerable considerations should be considered.
- Apparently, his pain is worse with breathing.

- The details of his outpatient treatment will not be summarized here, as they are well documented in a comprehensive copulation of his previous records.
- The patient had equal movement in all her legs.
- Mother realized she was pregnant at two months of age.
- If he wakes up, he is to have repeat doses of codeine plus lemon/honey/whiskey every 30 seconds in a steam room.
- She has never been married and I think was divorced.
- The patient was advised that if she could not awaken from sleep, she should call 911.
- The baby was discharged to home after being given written and verbal instructions.
- The patient's vision is 20.20 in both ears.
- When asked which knee was operated on, he cannot recall, but he notes that whichever knee it was, he still has a problem with it.
- Her implants were placed somewhere else.
- The patient is a very active and independent liver.
- The risks and benefits have been explained to the children of a CT scan.
- She usually has a bowel movement three times a day following meals and diarrhea.
- On examination, the testicles and penises are normal.
- He has a long history of a short leg.
- The patient refused an autopsy.
- Testicles are missing on this woman.
- The patient has no past history of suicides.
- Patient has two teenage children, but no other abnormalities.
- Heart problem is fixed. Patient died at 10:07 this morning.
- If it weren't for the fact that the patient is dead, I would say he was in perfect health.
- At this time he was felling trees, and in the process of a tree falling on another tree, he was hit by a tree and thrown face first against another tree.
- The patient was to have a bowel resection. However, he took a job as a stockbroker instead.

THE PREMEDICATED
HUMOR HALL OF FAME

- The left leg became numb at times, and she walked it off.
- The patient states there is a burning pain in his penis which goes to his feet.
- She has no rigors or shaking chills, but her husband states she was very hot in bed last night.
- Experienced mood swings because she suffered from PBS.
- The patient was bitten by a bat as he walked down the street on his thumb.

Able to do the worst possible job

Give Me a Sign

The most uncorrectable typographical error in history was perpetrated by William Safire, now the highly respected language columnist for the *New York Times*. In 1969, he got involved along with others in deciding what was to be inscribed on a bronze plaque that was to be deposited on the Moon—as soon as the first men set foot there. The team, including Safire, didn't know the date when the event would happen, so they went with the month only. So "July 1969, A.D." is what he told the plaque-maker to inscribe.

And that's what is still there.

Later Mr. Safire learned that although B.C. goes after the date, A.D. should come before. In a century or so, he writes in his book *Coming to*

Terms, he hopes some descendant of his will take a sharp stylus on some weekend transfer rocket trip to Mars via the Moon and use it to draw a little circle around the A.D. and then sketch a line to indicate that the circled "A.D." should go in front of "July."

Here on Earth, we experience the time of the signs that turn out to be signs of the times. These are less serious than the lunatic error on the Moon—and a lot funnier. In San Diego, where I live, I have spotted and cackled at the likes of "Semi-Live Entertainment" (doesn't sound very lively), "$16.00 adult admission. Children under 12 free. Limit one per family" (sounds like birth control in China), and, on the I-5 North freeway, erected by our highway department for the nautically challenged: "Cruise Ships Use Airport Exit."

Under a sign that was printed as "Doors Are Alarmed," some clever wag scrawled, "And the Windows Are Frightened." Have a look at these alarming sounds from around our land:

- *In a Winston-Salem, North Carolina, restaurant:* Shoes are required to eat inside.
- *Outside a Cardiff, California, restaurant:* Help keep the birds healthy. Don't feed them restaurant food.
- *In a Nova Scotia travel office:* Don't take a chance on ruining your vacation—come to us and be sure.
- *In a Kansas City oculist's office:* Broken lenses duplicated here
- *On a Lockhart, Texas, gas station and minimart:* We're out of Rolaids, but we've got gas.
- *In a Brooklyn barbershop window:* During construction we will shave you in the rear.
- *On a Rapid City, South Dakota, store:* Give That Bride a Good Case of Worms and Other Fine Bait.
- *On a San Diego farmers' market:*

> GIANT BLUEBERRIES
>
> SQUASH
>
> NATIVE CORN

- *Posted by the Boston Fire Department:*

> ```
> HYDRANT
> B.F.D.
> ```

- *On a newspaper rack in Melville, New York:* Please pay for newspapers before being taken.
- *On a building in Houston:* Christian Pest Control
- *Outside a Grand Rapids furniture store:* We promise you the lowest prices and workmanship.
- *On a gas pump in San Antonio:* Prepay In Advance Before Pumping.
- *In a Dayton barbershop:* During vacation, a competent hair stylist will be here.
- *In a Manhattan department store at Christmas:* Visit Santa's grotto. No waiting. We're the only store in New York with three Santas.
- *In a Las Vegas doctor's office:* Amnesia patients may have to pay in advance.
- *Outside a Plano, Texas, dry cleaning store:* Ten-minute parking for cleaning customers only
- *Sign outside Phoenix racecourse:* Live Horse Racing Today
- *In Oak Harbor, Washington:* Accident Prone Intersection. Caution.
- *In a pediatrician's office in Winterset, Iowa:* Do to accidental reasons, please pick up toys when finished. Thank you.
- *Outside a Los Angeles nail salon:* Nails in Rear
- *Outside a Van Nuys, California, gift shop:* Live Artificial Trees
- *Outside a Memphis, Tennessee, skating rink:* Rollerskate for Health. *Inside same rink:* Skate at Your Own Risk.
- *In Purchase, New York:* Purchase Free Library
- *Two signs found posted next to each other in a Wethersfield, Connecticut, country kitchen:* Restrooms/Please wait for hostess to seat you.
- *In front of a Concord, New Hampshire, restaurant:* Now serving live lobsters

- *On the menu of an Atlanta restaurant:* Blackened bluefish
- *In a Bar Harbor, Maine, restaurant:* Open seven days a week and weekends
- *In a Detroit restaurant:* Toilet out of order. Please use floor below.
- *On a Holiday Inn in Hyannis, Massachusetts:* Sleep with someone you know.
- *At a Houston ATM machine:* If you are blind, please use the Braille keys.
- *On the gate of a Londonderry, New Hampshire, farm:* For Sale: Eggs & Milk from Local Cows
- *On a Washington, D.C., building:* Spay/Neuter Clinic. Department of Human Services.
- *In a Bethesda, Maryland, country club:* Restrooms closed except for special events
- *On a Charleston, West Virginia, school property:* No Trespassing Without Permission
- *In an Orlando safari park:* Elephants Please Stay in Your Car.
- *In a parking lot in Los Angeles:*

COMPACT

TEACHERS

ONLY

- *On a gate in a Vail, Colorado, ski resort:* Going beyond this point may result in death and/or loss of skiing privileges.

Lest you think that only the United States is sign-disabled, have a look at these signs from other English-speaking countries:

- *On the wall of a Vancouver cleaning service:* Able to do the worst possible job
- *Attached to a chair in a Toronto hardware store:* Are your bottoms sagging? We provide a caning service.

- *Near an old folks home in a small English village:* Warning! Old people: Please don't make unnecessary noise.
- *In a British laundromat:* Automatic washing machines. Please remove all your clothes when the light goes out.
- *On many WCs in London:* Ladies, Gentlemen & Disabled Toilets
- *In a London department store:* Bargain Basement Upstairs
- *In an office in Shrewsbury:* Would the person who took the stepladder yesterday please bring it back, or further steps will be taken.
- *Outside a secondhand shop in Bath:* We exchange anything—bicycles, washing machines, etc. Why not bring your wife along and get a wonderful bargain?
- *In the northern countryside:* QUICKSAND WARNING: Any person passing this point will be drowned. By order of the District Council.
- *In a health food shop window:* Closed due to illness
- *In a dry cleaner's window:* Anyone leaving their garments here for more than 30 days will be disposed of.
- *In a London dance hall:* Smarts is the most exclusive disco in town. Everyone welcome.
- *At a London zoo:* Please do not feed the elephants. If you have any peanuts or buns, give them to the keeper on duty.
- *In a Manchester cemetery:* We must ask anyone with relatives buried in the graveyard to do their best to keep them in order.
- *On the fence of a rural farm:* The farmer allows walkers to cross the field for free, but the bull charges.
- *On a shop in Gloucester:* We can repair anything. (Please knock hard on the door. The bell doesn't work.)
- *In a Manchester shop:*

> CUSTOMERS SHOULD NOTE
> THAT ANY COMPLAINTS OF INCIVILITY
> ON THE PART OF OUR STAFF
> WILL BE SEVERELY DEALT WITH

THE SIGNS HALL OF FAME

- Eat here and get gas.
- Ears pierced while you wait
- Trespassers will be violated.
- Please wait for hostess to be seated.

```
NO
DOGS
EATING
BICYCLES
```

A World of
Errors

The
drinking water
in this airport
has been passed
by the
Quarantine
Authorities.

Towers of Babble

Inglish is the closest thing we have to a universal language since Latin in the days of the Roman Empire. Somewhere between 700 million and a billion people around the world speak English. At least they try to.

The novelist John Steinbeck's best-known book is *The Grapes of Wrath*. Steinbeck's wife liked to go into bookstores to look for books written by her husband. Once, when in Japan, she asked a bookstore clerk if the store carried any of his books. After checking, the clerk said, "Yes, we have *Angry Raisins*." The response brought forth laughter, not wrath, from Mrs. Steinbeck.

We venture abroad because we enjoy discovering differences. Travel can be hard work, as any road warrior will tell you. But travel can be fun, too, especially if you are open to the fractured English of the country you are visiting. One of the many pleasures of travel is that of reading and hearing Tinglish, or "tourist English," the developing world language of tourism to which postwar air travel has given such a tremendous boost.

- In the 1960s, tourists in Leningrad encountered this sign: "This is Leningrad Airport, and you are welcome to it."
- In the Shanghai Airport you will still see the sign "The drinking water in this airport has been passed by the Quarantine Authorities."
- An Indian guidebook informs the tourist that "Emperor Jehangir had 7,000 ladies in the harem. As he was a talented drunkard and a luxurious man, he died in 1627 at the age of 57."
- In front of a Taiwanese art museum stands a sign reading, "Close to Open."
- On election day in Bangkok was posted a warning, "No Beer Sold on Erection Day."
- A sign in Florence, Italy, cautions, "You are in a monumental palace, alike an Ufizzi's galley of Florence. You are therefore kindly requested to behave consequently."

English is spoken widely, but not always well. It is universally acknowledged by international students of our language that English is tough stuff—dotted with potholes, pitfalls, and pratfalls for the second-language speaker and writer, even the self-proclaimed expert. Consider these advertisements from professional interpreters:

- Are you unable to express you in English? I can help you in the right earnest!
- We guarantee strickly confidentiality.
- I do professional translations from and to English, Spanish, French, and Creole. I don't use softwares, and get you a job that is grammatically, and syntaxically perfect.

And consider these foreign commercial messages broadcast from the Tower of Babble:

- *Adorning a building in Yokosaka, Japan:* Beauty Saloon
- A sign in Cairo, Egypt, advertises a donkey ride for tourists: "Would you like to ride on your own ass?"

- An herbalist's catalogue in Venice advertises, "Make Thin! Obesity is a well known trouble. Fat people must not take around a majestic fatness, wearing large suits, perspirating too much."
- A sign outside a Turkish bath in Rome beckons, "Be pleased to come lie down with our masseuse. She will make you forget all your tired."
- Travelers to sun-drenched Amman, Jordan, are invited to cool off in "The Shadiest Cocktail Bar in Town."
- In the heart of the same downtown, a sign advises tourists to "Visit our bargain basement—one flight up." Enter and you will find "Pork Handbags" on sale.
- The wrapper of an ice-cream bar made in Russia cautions, "Do not taste our Ice Cream when it is too hard. Please continue your conversation until the Ice Cream grows into a softer. By adhering this advisement you will fully appreciate the wonderful Soviet Ice Cream."
- An Israeli professor advertised, "41, with 18 years of teaching in my behind. Looking for American-born woman who speaks English very good."
- A want-ad in an Indian newspaper made this unusual offer: "For sale to kind master: Full grown tigress, goes daily walk untied, and eats flesh from hand."
- In the window of a Hong Kong costume shop the merchandise is to be used "for turning tricks on Halloween."

Few are the travelers who have not, at one time or another, chuckled at a botched translation they've encountered somewhere abroad. More often than not, the Tinglish error—and the English terror—have leapt out of a hotel brochure or sign:

- *In a Kualapembuang, Indonesia, travel agency brochure:* Far up the river your journey is through mostly primary forest with impenetrable undergrowth, Giant Orchids, Mangrove flowers, huge tress with puthon crapping for branches and tropical bulfrongs.
- *In a promotional folder for a resort at Iguaco Falls, Brazil:* We offer you peace and seclusion. The paths to our resort are only passable by asses. Therefore, you will certainly feel at home here.
- *From an Italian holiday brochure:* Having freshly taken over the

propriety of this notorious house, I am wishful that you remove to me your esteemed costume. Standing among savage scenery, the hotel offers stupendous revelations. There is a French widow in ever bedroom, affording delightful prospects. I give personal look to the interior wants of each guest. Here, you shall be well fed up and agreeably drunk.

- *In an Indonesian hotel:* Someday Laundry Service
- *In a Bulgarian hotel:* If you are satisfactory, tell your friends. If you are unsatisfactory, warn the waitress.
- *In a Barcelona hotel courtyard:* No automobils. Pederasts only.
- *Hotel notice in Istanbul, Turkey:* Flying water in all room. You may bask in sin on patio.
- *In the rooms of another Istanbul hotel:* To call the room service, please open door and call Room Service.
- *In a Seville, Spain, hotel:* Those to require bathing please to notice the chambermaid.
- *Poster in Torremolinos, Spain:* Tabu Discotheque with or without a date and in summer—plus open air banging-bar
- *In a Cairo hotel:* On September 30, winter timing will start. As of 12:00 midnight all clocks will be forward one hour back.
- *In an African hotel:* You may choose between: a room with a view on the sea or the backside of the country.
- *In a Madrid hotel:* If you wish disinfection enacted in your presence, please cry out for the chambermaid.
- *In a Sorrento, Italy, hotel:* The concierge immediately for informations. Please don't wait last minutes. Then it will be too late to arrange any inconveniences.
- *In a Tuscany hotel brochure:* This hotel is renowned for its peace and solitude. In fact, crowds from all over the world flock here to enjoy its solitude.
- *In a hotel brochure, Amalfi, Italy:* Suggestive views from every window
- *In a hotel brochure, Zurich, Switzerland:* We have nice bath and are very good in bed.
- *On hotel TV set in Belgrade, Yugoslavia:* If set breaks, inform manager. Do not interfere with yourself.
- *Posted in another Yugoslavian hotel:* Let us know about an unficiency as well as leaking on the service. Out utmost will improve it.

• *In a Budapest hotel room:* All rooms not denounced by twelve o'clock will be paid for twicely.

• *In a Leipzig, Germany, hotel room:* Ladies, please rinse out your teapots standing upside down in sink. In no event should hot bottoms be placed on the counter.

• *Notice posted on every floor of a Florence, Italy, hotel:* Fire! It is what we can doing we hope. No fear. Not ourselves. Say quietly to all people coming up down everywhere a prayer. Always is a clerk. He is assured of safety by expert men who are in the bar for telephone for the fighters of the fire come out.

Finally, gaze upon these two responses to inquiries for accommodations abroad:

• Dear Madam: I am honorable to accept your impossible request. Unhappy it is I have not bedroom with bath. A bathroom with bed I have. I can though give you a washing, with pleasure, in a most clean spring with no one to see. I insist that you will like this.

• Dear Madam: I am amazingly diverted by your entreaty for a room. I can offer you a commodious chamber with balcony imminent to romantic gorge, and I hope you will want to drop in. A vivacious stream washes my doorsteps, so do not concern yourself that I am not too good in bath. I am superb in bed.

With education standards around the world constantly rising, it is perhaps inevitable that Tinglish will one day become a dead language. But I hope that for at least a few more years adventurers traveling abroad will be instructed to "leave values at the front desk" and "not to have children in the bar."

THE HOTEL SIGNS HALL OF FAME

- *In a Tokyo hotel:* Is forbitten to steal hotel towels please. If you are not person to do such thing is please not to read notis.
- *At a French Riviera hotel swimming pool:* Swimming is forbidden in the absence of a savior.
- *In a Beirut hotel:* Ladies are kindly requested not to have their babies in the cocktail bar.
- *In a Belgrade hotel:* The flattening of underwear with pleasure is the job of the chambermaid.
- *In a Kyoto, Japan, hotel:* You are invited to take advantage of the chambermaid.

Frayed Chicken

Unappetizing Menus

On a Chinese menu you can read, "Mr. Zheng and his fellowworkers like to meet you and entertain you with their hostility and unique cooking techniques."

A Warsaw restaurant advertises with the exultation "As for the tripe served here, you will be singing its praises to your grandchildren on your deathbed."

A menu in a Swiss restaurant boasts, "Our wines leave you nothing to hope for."

A Shanghai Mongolian hot pot buffet guarantees, "You will be able to eat all you wish until you are fed up!"

An Indian restaurant advertises, "Our establishment serves tea in a bag like mother."

A Tel Aviv hotel advertises its room service, "If you wish for breakfast, lift our telephone, and the waitress will arrive. This will be enough to bring your food up."

An Italian menu requests that you "Please pay the house waiter the price of your consummation."

A hotel notice in Ankara, Turkey, announces, "You are invite to visit our restaurant where you can eat the Middle East Foods in a European ambulance."

A restaurant in Indonesia's Jakarta Hilton beckons customers with this come-on: "Grill and Roast Your Clients!"

On a "Family Style" restaurant in Hong Kong appears the sign "Come Broil Yourself at Your Own Table."

A Tokyo restaurant requests that you "Please do not bring outside food, excluding children under five."

And a Japanese steak house boasts of its house specialty thus: "Teppan Yaki—before your cooked right eyes."

If you travel a lot, you know that some of the most memorable experiences can occur in restaurants and that some of the most memorable "English" appears on foreign menus. Eating in a foreign restaurant can be a genuine adventure spiced by culinary and linguistic entertainment.

One restaurant in Rome listed on its menu "Mixed Boils to Pick." The Italian phrase is simply "mixed boiled meats of your choosing," a tasty dish of simmered beef, veal, chicken, tongue, and sausages. But something got lost in translation. Italian eggplant is *melanzane*. Some conscientious translator searched English dictionaries and found that *mela* means "apple" in English and *zane* means "nutty or crazy." So eggplant in Italy is often listed as "Mad Apples."

Here is an imaginary menu consisting of skewed and skewered items spotted by tourists around the world. Most will tell you that the choice of such dishes has livened up their meals abroad. Yum.

WHORES DOVER

SOUP

Gritty Balloons in Soup   Fisherman's Crap Soup

Barely Soup   Soap of the Day

Limpid Red Beet Soup with

Cheesy Dumplings in the Form of a Finger

SALAD

Salad, a Firm's Own Make   Groin Salad

MEAT

Buff Steak   Gut Casserole

Warm Little Dogs   Hambugger

Calf Pluck   Dreaded Veel Cutlets

Roast Beast   Pork with Fresh Garbage

Sir Loin Steak   Boiled Sheep

Sour Pig's Fore Shank   Special Big Leg

Live Wurst   Meat Dumping

Beef Rashers Beaten Up in

the Country People's Fashion

Tortilla Topped with Chili, Melted Cheese,

Sour Cream, and Glaucoma

SEAFOOD

Muscles in Sailor's Sauce   Drunken Prawns in Spit

Shrimp in a Casket

Dead Shrimp on Warm Vegetables

Sea Blubber in a Spicy Sauce

POULTRY

Chicken Low Mein

Hen Fried with Butler

Bosom of Chicken

Foul Breast

Frayed Chicken

Goose Barnacles

Sweat from the Turkey

Roasted Duck Let Loose

Utmost of Chicken Fried in Bother

Lightly Flowered Breast of Chicken

Utmost of Chicken with Smashed Pot

MISCELLANEOUS OR UNIDENTIFIABLE

Pasta Fungus

Baked Zit

Spleen Omelet

Children Sandwich

Eight Treasurers

Buttered Saucepans

Mixed Boils to Pick

Muffled Frog Rumps

Anti Pasta

Slugs in Spit

Bird Bowels

Withered Peper Paste Sauce

Toes with Butter and Jam

Cold Shredded Children

Fried Hormones

Fried Convoluted Watch

Spaghetti Fongoole

Full Coarse Meal

VEGETABLES

Priest Fainted Eggplant Dish

Muchrooms

Backed Beans

Mushed Potatoes

Potato Cheeps

Fried Rice from Hell

Cabitch

Raped Carrots

French Fried Ships

Mad Apples

DESSERTS

Pie Tongue	Honey Do
Tart of the House	Strawberry Crap
Chocolate Mouse Tort	Lady's Finger
Finest Moldy Cheese	Chocolate Sand Cookies

Pustache Ice Cream

Fire Pudding with Hard Sauce

Rice Kooky

BEVERAGES

White Whine	Cock and Tail
Fried Milk	Lemon Jews
Turkey Coffee	Garlic Coffee

Floating Iceberg

Special Cocktails for Women with Nuts

THE GLOBAL GABBLE HALL OF FAME

This is an "English" synopsis of Act One of *Carmen,* exactly as it appeared in the program of a theater in Genoa, Italy:

Carmen is a cigar-makeress from a tabago factory who loves Don José of the mounting guard. Carmen takes a flower from her corsets and lances it to Don José. (Duet: "Talk me of my mother.") There is a noise inside the tabago factory and the revolting cigar-makeresses burst into the stage. Carmen is arrested and Don José is ordered to mounting guard her but Carmen subduces him and he lets her escape.

Tounge of Frog

Beware Tounge of Frog

As a foreigner, one of the first things you notice in Japan is all the wacky English on toys, appliances, and food and beverage containers. Most product packaging in Japan has at least some English, although you'll probably find it more amusing than useful. Occidental tourists find this crazy and colorful English a little curious.

So why all the odd translations? One Canadian teaching English in Japan tells a story about a woman who was taking one of his basic English courses. This is the class for people with little or no knowledge of the English language. Talking to the class in halting English, a student explained what she did at work all day—write the English captions on Japanese drink cans.

This explains why a sign at a Japanese electronics shop reads, "You want it, we had it," and why a Japanese road sign announces inexplicably, "Try bigger and bigger but keep more and more slowly."

On a Greek ferry: In case of emergency, passengers will proceed to muster stations following yellow arrows wearing life jackets.

On a Vietnamese boat: Nobody is allowed to sit on both sides of the boat.

An instructive classic is the Taiwanese English text of "Tounge of Frog." Some people actually buy this product so that they can chuckle at the accompanying instructions:

INSTRUCTIONS FOR
TOUNGE OF FROG

A product has the stickness and is just like a soft rubber band with high contractility. It can be played to stick the remote objects. If it is thrown will full of your strength, it will spit out the tounge, which is like the genuine one from a frog.

Inspite of it is sticky, it is never like the chewing guns which is glued tightly and cannot be separated.

The key point for throwing far away is the same as the throwing of fish rod, i.e. to separate it with two hands, then release one hand and to throw out slowly with full of your strength.
CAUTIONS:

Never throw out the other person's head.

Inspite of it is nontoxic, it cannot be eaten.

Its content has the oil, so if it touches on cloth, precious object, or wall, the stains will remain if you don't care about it.

These helpful hints were displayed in a Le Touquet hotel in 1932:

INSTRUCTIONS TO USERS OF
THE ASCENSEUR

Persons ignorant of the manoeuvres of the Ascenseur are prayed instantly to address themselfs to the concierge—

Never attempt to mount the Ascenseur nor to get out before having constated the absolute arrest of the cabine. If the cabine is in march or stopped at a stage, be certain that the people who are found there have quitted it. Once in the cabine, shut, with care, all the portals, then command the manoeuvres by leaning on the button of the stage where one wants to render oneself and eventually on the button of mounting.

In course of the route, never touch the portals of the cabine. Their overture can provoke the arrest of the cabine. One must, if the cabine produces itself by mistake or inattention, reclose with pain the open portals and command anew the manoeuvres like at the departure.

In case of tempestuous stop in course of the march, open the portals and close at once, and command descent by leaning on the button and eventually, on the button of descent.

Now gaze upon the directions on a box containing an artificial Christmas tree, made in China:

USE AND MAINTENANCE

After take off the package, you will see that the shape of the tree body will be in a unnormal shape statue. But this is because of it still in the package statue. So before you set the fiber optic X'mas tree, you should reorganize the tree by manual up you satisfy with its shape.

To use, please insert the output plug of the power transformer into the input jack of the flower pot first. Then input the flower case at the end of the tree body into the related hole on the flower pot. The switch is on the bottom flower pot. Turn it to on. After that, put the X'mas tree on the table or ground and switch on. Then can you watch and enjoy its dreamlike appearance. If you watch in a deem light or at the night, it will be much splendid.

Please turn off when there will be nobody around for a long time.

Some lovers of loopy lingo have been known to buy a Japanese-made vegetable chopper for the instructions, rather than the product itself:

MULTI-CHOPPER

In order that the article has minced could be perfectly cut, Knocked Vigorously on the bud Superior hand Opened. The more or less great number of chops determines the fineness of cup. The rotation of knives is made automatically and regularly.

For the cleaning, to pull the inferior bell and to release the recipient Superior. Well to rinse the machine, if possible to the running water. Re-assembly in Senses inverts. All parts metallic are executed in materials has the test of rust.

THE INSTRUCTIVE HALL OF FAME

Japanese Rules of the Road

1. At the rise of the hand of the policeman, stop rapidly. Do not pass him, otherwise disrespect him.

2. When passenger of the foot heave in sight, tootle the horn trumpet melodiously at first. If he still obstacles your passage, tootle with vigor and express by word of mouth the warning "Hai. Hai."

3. Beware of the wandering horse that he shall not take fright as you pass him. Do not explosion the exhaust pipe. Go soothingly by him or stop by the roadside till he pass away.

4. Give big space to the festive dog that make sport in the roadway. Avoid entanglement with your wheel spoke.

5. Go soothingly on the grease mud as there lurk the skid demon.

6. Try bigger and bigger, but press more and more dainty.

7. Press the brake of the foot as you roll around the corner to save the collapse and tires.

Press Messes

4-H girls win prizes for fat calves.

Heading for Trouble

Everybody makes mistakes. But when headline writers make theirs, the results scream out to hundreds of thousands of readers in big, black, inch-high print. Headlines are what your eyes catch first when you pick up your newspaper. Sometimes those headlines are just plain funny and detonate your stomach into a rolling boil, as when the *Los Angeles Times* announced:

> EX-GOP HOPEFUL HUFFINGTON
> SAYS HE IS A HOMOSEXUAL
> HE ALSO SAYS HE MAY BE A DEMOCRAT

Writing headlines is an art in itself. To make the size of the head-lines fit the page layout is an artistic challenge. To say whatever it is you have and want to say in exactly the space and type size you have at your disposal is a veritable architectural feat.

This task is usually done by subeditors, who labor in obscurity. They have one of the most difficult jobs in journalism, yet their work goes un-recognized—until one of their mangled headlines gets sent to me. Then, if the headline is really loopy enough, I make it famous and infamous in these pages.

Take (please!) the following headline from the *Boston Globe*:

DELAY: DON'T RUSH TO CENSURE

You might do a double take with that one until you read the open-ing paragraph, which describes the maneuvers involved in the proposed censure of President Bill Clinton: "House majority whip Tom DeLay urged senators Wednesday not to rush into a censure deal but 'to spend plenty of time in the evidence room' with prosecutors' materials. If they do, he said, the 67 votes for President Clinton's removal 'may appear out of thin air.'"

As a veteran head(line)-hunter I have a number of examples of these two-headed headlines among my trophies. Our sprawling English language has more words with two or more meanings than any other lan-guage. Note how the double meaning of a word or two creates delicious confusion in each of the following banner bloopers:

4-H GIRLS WIN PRIZES FOR FAT CALVES

◎

MOWRY FALLS APART, SHOOTS 85

◎

BIG BUSTS INDICATE
DRUG WAR WORKING

◎

CONCRETE STEP TAKEN

⊚

PRESIDENT CLINTON'S PROBLEMS ARE MOUNTING

⊚

GIANT WOMEN'S STUDY SHORT OF VOLUNTEERS

⊚

JUDGE PRESSES JACKSON'S SUIT

⊚

ASTRONAUT TAKES BLAME
FOR GAS IN SPACECRAFT

⊚

BROADCASTERS TO LOOK
INTO PLUNGING GOWNS

⊚

MARCH PLANNED FOR NEXT AUGUST

⊚

BREAKING WIND COULD CUT COSTS

⊚

CASE OF STOLEN WHISKEY
EXPECTED TO GO TO JURY

⊚

BLIND BISHOP APPOINTED TO SEE

⊚

LINGERIE SHIPMENT HIJACKED—
THIEF GIVES POLICE THE SLIP

⊚

FRESHMEN WOMEN OUTSTRIP MEN AT I.U.

❂

L.A. VOTERS APPROVE URBAN RENEWAL BY LANDSLIDE

❂

OUTHOUSES AIRED AT COUNCIL MEETING

❂

FOR FORTY YEARS HE PLAYED WITH
HIS WIFE ON VAUDEVILLE CIRCUITS

❂

BALLS, BALLS, BALLS
IS ALL DEBUTANTES GET

❂

BENTON WOMAN IS HOSPITALIZED BY ACCIDENT

❂

POLICE HOPE TO CALM FEARS OF STABBER

❂

GOOSE GIVEN TO EISENHOWER

❂

PATIENT AT DEATH'S DOOR—
DOCTORS PULL HIM THROUGH

❂

WOMEN SPEND MORE TIME
IN KITCHEN DESPITE ADVANCES

❂

JURY HUNG IN BRA CASE

❂

CROUPIERS ON STRIKE—
MANAGEMENT: "NO BIG DEAL"

◎

STADIUM AIR CONDITIONING FAILS—
FANS PROTEST

◎

WOMEN ARE URGED TO FLATTEN CANS

◎

FIVE NUDES PINCHED AT STAG SHOW

◎

ARMY FOCUSES ON SECOND BASE IN SEX PROBE

◎

BOARD FILLS HOLE IN POST

◎

BAR TRYING TO HELP ALCOHOLIC LAWYERS

◎

MARIJUANA ISSUE SENT TO JOINT COMMITTEE

◎

LACK OF SIZE DOES NOT DETER LEXINGTON'S PETERS

◎

SUPREME COURT CONSIDERS HOMOSEXUALITY

◎

HUMANA VOLUNTEERS TO FIGHT
AGAINST CHILDREN USING TOBACCO

◎

DOW HIGHER; HELPED BY DRUGS

⊚

WOMEN'S BODY SEEKS MEMBER

⊚

MAN HELD IN CLOTHING STORE FIRE

⊚

FRENCH DAM SITE BETTER OFF
WITH U.S. AID FUNDS

⊚

PRICK TESTING IS OPTIMAL
FOR MAKING LATEX ALLERGY DIAGNOSIS

Often the two-headed ambiguity results from a confusion about what part of speech a certain word is. In the headline MOOSE KILL 1,230, for example, is *kill* a noun or a verb? Did moose kill 1,230 people, or did people kill 1,230 moose?

JUDGE SELECTS DOCTORS
TO HELP IMPLANT JURORS

⊚

MAGISTRATE ORDERS SHOOTING
SUSPECT HELD WITHOUT BAIL

⊚

DOG OWNER ORDERED TO PAY
$1,000 TO BITE VICTIM

⊚

YELLOW PERCH DECLINE TO BE STUDIED

⊚

BOMB SNIFFING DOGS AT OLYMPICS

HIGH COURT HELPS RAPE VICTIMS

JAIL RELEASES UPSET JUDGES

JURY GETS DRUNK DRIVING CASE HERE

NATURE WALKS ON THURSDAY EVENINGS

RUSSIAN FORCES BEAR DOWN

NEW SATELLITE DATA HINT THAT
UNIVERSE MAY BE BIGGER THAN THOUGHT

HOME DEPOT PURCHASES
WALLPAPER, BLINDS RETAILERS

THE ESPECIALLY EMBARRASSING
HEADLINES HALL OF FAME

- During the 1934 World Series, St. Louis pitcher Dizzy Dean tried to break up a double play and was struck in the head by a relay throw. The force of the ball knocked him unconscious, and sent the daffy pitcher to the hospital. Luckily Dean was not injured. The next day, a headline read, X-RAYS OF DEAN'S HEAD REVEAL NOTHING.

- Advances by the Allied forces in World War II were headlined in one newspaper as ALLIES PUSH BOTTLE UP 10,000 GERMANS.

- On the morning of the Illinois–Ohio State football game, when Illinois would have to play without the services of its star running back, Frosty Peters, a newspaper published this beauty: ILLINI FACE BUCKS WITH FROSTY PETERS OUT.

- A famous *Boston Globe* headline asked this scientific question: IS THERE A RING OF DEBRIS AROUND URANUS?

- The *Saturday Evening Post* ran an article written by the wife of a billiards professional. She told how part of her job as her husband's assistant was to make sure that the billiard balls were exactly at room temperature. The subheadline appeared as SHE KEEPS HIS BALLS WARM.

MEN BURST IN HOME, STEAL CASH

Having Your Head(lines) Examined

More than 50 years ago, editor E. P. Mitchell lamented, "There is no livelier perception in newspaper offices than of the incalculable havoc being wreaked upon the language by the absurd circumstance that only so many millimeters of type can go into so many millimeters width of column." Sometimes those constructions produce penetrating glimpses into the obvious: When headlines blare, RESEARCHERS CALL MURDER A THREAT TO PUBLIC SAFETY and FEDERAL AGENTS RAID GUN SHOP, FIND WEAPONS, we are likely to blink and say, "Huh?"

A headline howler from the Potomac, Virginia, *News* blared: MEN BURST IN HOME, STEAL CASH.

Huh? Did these fellows rob the place before or after they exploded? The cleanup must have been quite a messy job. The headline should have read, MEN BURST INTO HOME. . . .

In BOY HURT IN ACCIDENT IN INTENSIVE CARE, the reader may ask, "Did two gurneys collide?" Gazing at ELIGIBLE PET OWNERS CAN GET FREE NEUTERING, the reader may ask, "Who's getting neutered?"

The Poughkeepsie *Journal* ran a science headline announcing SCIENTISTS GROW FROG EYES, EARS. The article that followed explained that frog embryo cells cultured in a solution of retinoic acid develop into entire organs, either eyes or ears according to the concentration.

A St. Louis woman, born on February 29, gave birth to a daughter exactly 20 years later. In the early edition, the St. Louis *Post-Dispatch* headline announced: WOMAN BORN FEBRUARY 29 HAS BABY SAME DAY.

Huh? We've heard of preternaturally mature women, but . . .

Here are some more classic blinkers:

MORNING SICKNESS LINKED TO GENDER

◎

THREE MORE MOONS FOUND ON NEPTUNE

◎

FOR NINTH TIME IN 2 YEARS,
LEOMINSTER TEEN DIES VIOLENTLY

◎

MINERS REFUSE TO WORK AFTER DEATH

◎

GRANDSON BORN TO JACK BENNY

◎

EIGHT AMERICAN MEN LEFT

⊚

AUTOS KILLING 110 A DAY;
LET'S RESOLVE TO DO BETTER

⊚

VERMONTER SAYS MORE
SKIING GOES ON IN WINTER

⊚

SANTA ROSA MAN DENIES
HE COMMITTED SUICIDE IN SAN FRANCISCO

⊚

MOTORMAN WELL AUTOPSY REVEALS

⊚

BOYS AND GIRLS SAME ALL OVER

⊚

MAN IS CHARGED WITH KILLING HIS MISSING WIFE

⊚

NEVADA HAS WATER BUT IT CAN'T BE USED UNTIL FOUND

⊚

NONBELIEVERS GATHER TO SHARE THEIR BELIEFS

⊚

FBI TO ASSIST POLICE IN LOWELL ROBBERY

⊚

TWO-HEADED BABY RECALLS
SIMILAR BIRTH IN 1970

⊚

DEATH CAUSES CHANGE

✇

WIFE'S FAMILY: MAN WHO KILLED
FAMILY NOT ALL GOOD

✇

MOTHER OF ALL DEADBEAT DADS
GETS 6 MONTHS IN PRISON

It's not easy to hit the nail on the headline when composing a 60-point statement that accurately conveys the content of a story and fits into the allotted space:

HEADLESS BODY FOUND IN TOPLESS BAR

✇

CHIEF THROWS HIS HEART INTO HELPING FEED NEEDY

✇

FORECLOSURE LISTINGS: ENTIRE STATE OF N.J. AVAILABLE

✇

SEVERED HEAD OFFERS FEW ANSWERS

✇

737 FROM BOSTON HIT BY LIGHTNING

✇

MAN EXECUTED AFTER LONG SPEECH

✇

PLEA FOR CUT IN PRICE OF FREE MILK

✇

BATH OFFICER SHOOTS MAN WITH KNIFE

※

MILLION WOMAN MARCH
ATTRACTS THOUSANDS

※

EXPERTS INCREASE PROBABILITY
OF A BIG QUAKE IN CALIFORNIA

※

FIREPROOF CLOTHING FACTORY BURNS TO GROUND

※

TYPHOON RIPS CEMETERY
HUNDREDS DEAD

And what havoc can be wreaked by a wrong word or mixed-up metaphor:

LASER SURGERY AVAILABLE FOR PROSTRATE

※

THREE LADIES INDICTED INTO THE HALL OF FAME

※

WIDESPREAD EATING DISORDERS
GNAW AT ARGENTINA'S YOUNG

※

AMERICAN AIRLINES EXPECTS
TO BE BACK ON TRACK BY WEEKEND

No newspaper can protect its borders against the invasion of the illegal spelling gremlins. Newsman Bob Consodine chuckled with the memory of having written a story about a blond player named Don Mc-Neill, who won the U.S. tennis championship. He wrote his lead as

"Tow-headed Don McNeill today won . . ." It appeared in the *New York Mirror* as "Two-headed Don McNeill . . ."

The *Montreal Herald* scurried around like crazy calling back early editions of the paper after a famous British ship arrived. The reason was a misspelling in the head: ELECTRIC GIRDLE ON QUEEN ELIZABETH IS NAVEL SECRET.

THE HEADLINE HOWLERS
HALL OF FAME

GRANDMOTHER OF EIGHT
MAKES HOLE IN ONE

FLAMING TOILET SEAT CAUSES
EVACUATION AT HIGH SCHOOL

BRITISH UNION FINDS
DWARFS IN SHORT SUPPLY

MAN STRUCK BY LIGHTNING
FACES BATTERY CHARGE

FRIED CHICKEN IN MICROWAVE
WINS FREE TRIP TO HAWAII

About 1 million antlered deer hunters were expected to take to the Pennsylvania woods for the first day of deer season.

Read My Clips

A lecturer on dress reform was shocked at the report of one of her speeches that appeared in the *Lakewood* (Ohio) *Times*. The story concluded with "the lady lecturer on dress reform wore nothing that was remarkable." But somewhere along the way from story to type, a period was inserted, so that the published version ended, "The lady lecturer on dress reform wore nothing. That was remarkable."

An AP story about Amy Fisher reported, "In 1992, Fisher, then 16, knocked on the door of Mrs. Buttafuoco's Massapequa home and shot her in the head. At the time, Fisher was having sex with Mrs. Buttafuoco's husband, Joey. He later served six months in jail for statutory rape."

Quite a balancing act.

A *Wall Street Journal* columnist warned, "President Clinton's temptation will be to grab the first fig leaf Mr. Milosevic offers, once the Serb has achieved what he wants on the ground in Kosovo."

We can imagine that Bill Clinton can find good use for fig leaves, but we suspect that the columnist confused "fig leaf" with "olive branch."

An article was headlined BRUSSELS PAYS 20,000 POUNDS TO SAVE PROSTITUTES. The report included this statement: "The money will not be going directly into the prostitutes' pockets, but will be used to encourage them to lead a better life. We will be training them for new positions in hotels."

Hmmm. What kind of positions?

It's hot-off-the-press gaffes like these that become material for stand-up comedians like Jay Leno, who ridicules headlines, articles, and ad copy. It's de-pressing how some newspapers strew about the verbal equivalent of banana peels for their readers to slip on. Culled from the nation's presses, here are some more slippery slips and sloppy slops:

• About 1 million antlered deer hunters were expected to take to the Pennsylvania woods for the first day of deer season.

• An animal-rights group that hopes to change Americans' meat-eating ways scheduled a meeting here today at the Black Angus steakhouse.

• Asked if they supported women's lib, 47.5 percent said they did, 44.3 percent said they did not, and 8.2 percent had no opinion. Broken down by sex, 48.9 percent of the men favored the movement, compared to only 45.4 percent of the women.

• Billy George Hughes, Jr., 47, had become a lightning rod for both sides of the capital punishment issue.

• Negotiations are proceeding for a February bout between the 21-year-old daughter of former heavyweight champion Muhammed Ali and Jane Couch in London.

• Smith was one of ten Dallas businessmen robbed and brutally beaten with aluminum baseball bats from October to January.

- Twice a bridegroom and finally a bride—at least for last night—was Suzanne Grazzione.

- The relationship between the two dormitory roommates had soured recently when the murder victim, stabbed 45 times, declared she would room with someone else next year.

- The Reverend Jeremy Sonnenfeld wants to visit many ministers, lay people in the 27 conference countries.

- We note with regret that Mr. Kramer is recovering after his serious operation.

- The main jail, near West Palm Beach, houses juveniles charged as adults and women.

- Paula Jones, shown at a Long Beach, California, news conference Tuesday, plans to attend President Clinton's deposition in sex suit.

- A young girl, who was blown out to sea on a set of inflatable teeth, was rescued by a man on an inflatable lobster. A coast-guard spokesman commented, "This sort of thing is all too common these days."

- Died. J. Duncan Parsons, 90, oil magnate; in Houston. Parsons' admirers were hoping that week that he would not be remembered primarily for last year's May–December 31st marriage to model Jan McMillan.

- Tom Mix and his wonder horse, Tony, are featured. In some stunts, Tom shows almost human intelligence.

- The witness claimed that he observed sex taking place between two parked cars.

- One victim was taken to Swedish Memorial Hospital. He suffered at least two broken legs.

- Governor Miller plans to ask lawmakers to boost funding to state colleges and universities by $259 million. He also wants to expand the $158 million lottery-funded kindergarten program by $42 to eliminate 10,000 children on the waiting list.

- "After finding no qualified candidates for the position of principal, the school department is extremely pleased to announce the appointment of Charles Stanton to the post," said Philip Stauffer, superintendent.

- The club's celebration will also include a DJ and balloons falling from the ceiling at midnight. "It's just going to be a bunch of people having a good time," said Dan Burris, owner of the Turf Club.

- Mr. and Mrs. Charles Cooper announce the betrayal of their daughter Miss Margaret to Ensign Raymond McKee.
- A bathroom shower was given the bride.
- Upon arriving at the Honolulu airport, two men were given coveted lays by Hawaiian maidens.
- Beginning this semester, references to women in any of the Student Association's writing have been discontinued. Instead, females will be referred to in a new, improved, non-sexist term: "womyn." "The idea is to take the 'men' out of 'women,' " explained Central Council chairperson Jeffrey Banks.
- Six men, their faces covered with red bandannas, got out of a Cherokee carrying a knife, baseball bat, billy club, and rolling pin, said Davis, 20. "I knew when I saw the rolling pin that something bad was going down," Davis said.
- We suggest that senior citizens buy automobiles with power steering, automatic transmission, and power brakes and install special mirrors to extend their view if they have problems turning their heads 360 degrees.
- A twister roared through the area today, leaving three people dead and counting.
- Woody is the father of eight children and nine grandchildren.
- Happy Buc fans ate 41,000 hot dogs at a recent double header drawing 32,346 fans. Also 27,000 bags of peanuts, 26,000 ice cream bars, 30,000 soft drinks, 18,000 score cards, and 7,500 cushions.
- Obituary: She was known for her heart of gold, always giving of herself and never expecting anything in return. She enjoyed talking with people, cooking her infamous lasagna meals, walking, reading, and bowling.
- A 56-year-old man died Monday afternoon after he apparently ran a stop sign, struck a sedan, and vaulted into a minivan.
- At the Knights of Columbus dinner they will serve the same fish as last year.
- Winners at the card party were Miss Wilma Schmidt, a turkey, and Mrs. Ethel Riggs, a chicken.
- The first time that Sharita Lawrence spotted lice on one of her daughter's heads, she remained calm because she knew the drill.

- Ancestors of Andrew Jackson will hold their biennial reunion in Nashville this weekend.

- At 15 Celsius, it was feared that people could not be stupid enough to attend these winter games in such bitter cold. But once again Calgarians have proven the experts wrong.

- The Chico, California, city council enacted a ban on nuclear weapons, setting a $500 fine for anyone detonating one within city limits.

- A Culver City cat was killed with a high-powered pellet gun Thursday afternoon, police said. Culver City police investigators are considering the feline's death suspicious.

- Some 40 percent of female gas station employees in Metro Detroit are women, up from almost 9 a year ago.

- The rape prevention course is a hands-on training and awareness session, to be offered in the Franklin Elementary School.

- Carrie Seltzer, 43, of Salem, suffered minor injury after a car she was riding in struck a cow crossing Western Reserve Rd., at 8:15 P.M. The car had to be destroyed by its owner.

- Members of the National Association of Letter Carriers fell short of the 50,000 pounds they collected last year, but said the food was a higher quality than last year. Letter carriers picked up canned nonperishable food left by mailboxes Saturday.

- Please put your trash inside the dumpsters. Adults are throwing cans, bottles, and trash down as well as children.

- John Masten, the celebrated singer, was in an automobile accident last week. We are happy to state that he was able to appear the following evening in four pieces.

- Lettuce won't turn brown if you put your head in a plastic bag before placing it in the refrigerator.

- An anonymous female caller reported that a parked car had earlier passed her going 100 miles per hour.

- What is more beautiful for a blonde to wear at formal dances than white tulle? My answer—and I'm sure you will agree with me—is "nothing."

THE GALLEY OOPS! HALL OF FAME

- The license fee for altered dogs with a certificate will be $3, and for pets owned by senior citizens who have not been altered the fee will be $1.50.
- Brian Porter, embezzler, endorsed checks for $90,299.77 last year. For nine months, he played the daily double, sipped dry martinis, dallied with expensive prostitutes, flew first class city to city, and spent the rest foolishly.
- This afternoon, firemen battled a skyscraper fire in New York. It was confined to the upper floor, where smoke bellowed from the windows.
- Political insiders call them wedge issues—raw, emotional issues like social security for Democrats and capital punishment for Republicans.

Lunch will be gin at 12:15 P.M.

The House of Corrections

A newspaper is a daily marvel, even a miracle. There are 1,730 of them published daily in the United States, with a combined circulation of nearly 62 million. Limitless possibilities exist for error, human and mechanical. Add the crushing pressure of deadlines, and it's surprising there aren't more mistakes.

When goofs pop off the page, editors scurry to print corrections, even though we often prefer the misprint to the corrected version. As the Van Buren (Arkansas) *Press-Argus* ruefully observed, "It's nearly as hard to correct a typographical error as it is to get a woman unpregnant."

• Instead of being arrested, as we stated, for kicking his wife down a flight of stairs and hurling a lighted kerosene lamp after her, the Reverend James P. Wellman died unmarried four years ago. (From a 19th-century American newspaper, quoted in an undated letter by Sir Edward Burne-Jones to Lady Homer.)

• The following typo appeared in our last community news announcement: "Lunch will be gin at 12:15 P.M." Please correct to read "12 noon."

• IMPORTANT NOTICE: If you are one of hundreds of parachuting enthusiasts who bought our *Easy Sky Diving* book, please make the following correction: on page 8, line 7, the words "state zip code" should have read "pull rip cord."

• In criticizing the political views of Patrick Buchanan, William Bennett said, "It's a real us-and-them kind of thing," not, as we reported, "It's a real S&M kind of thing."

• It was incorrectly reported last Friday that today is T-shirt Appreciation Day. In fact, it is actually Teacher Appreciation Day.

• The sermon at the Presbyterian Church this coming Sunday will be "There Are No Sects in Heaven." The subject was incorrectly printed in yesterday's edition as "There Is No Sex in Heaven."

• We apologize here to Neil Chernick, who has joined the staff of ChemSystems, based in Hong Kong, as an "executive consultant," not as an "expensive consultant," as we reported.

• There was a mistake in an item sent in two weeks ago which stated that Ed Burnham entertained a party at crap shooting. It should have been trap shooting.

• Miss Rumson has been appointed supervisor of Work Area Six, not (as stated in our August issue) Work Area Sex.

• We apologize to our readers who received, through an unfortunate computer error, the chest measurements of members of the Female Wrestlers Association instead of the figures on the sales of soybeans to foreign countries.

• In Frank Washburn's March column, Rebecca Varney was erroneously identified as a bookmaker. She is a typesetter.

• There are two important corrections to the information in the update on our Deep Relaxation professional development program. First, the program will include meditation, not medication. Second, it is experiential, not experimental.

• Our article about Jewish burial customs contained an error: Mourners' clothing is rent—that is, torn—not rented.

• In the City Beat section of Friday's paper, firefighter Dwight Brady was misidentified. His nickname in the department is "Dewey." Another firefighter is nicknamed "Weirdo." We apologize for our mistake.

• Because of an editing error, a front-page article yesterday about Ross Perot's acceptance speech as the Reform Party candidate for president misstated the date of the winter George Washington's troops spent in Valley Forge, Pennsylvania, a few miles from the convention site. It was 1777–78, not 1977–78.

• Just to keep the record straight, it was the famous Whistler's Mother, not Hitler's, that was exhibited. There is nothing to be gained in trying to explain how this error occurred.

• An April 5 story stated that Andrea Fratello did not return a reporter's calls seeking comment. Fratello died last December.

• A printing error last week caused confusion. The price for this smartly modernized semi-detached horse is $53,000.

• A story on Jennifer Corey Thursday incorrectly stated that the family of a missing girl came to her for a psychic consultation. Two friends of the girl came to that session, and later Corey talked with the girl's mother. Also Corey worked for Rutland Mental Health, not Rutland Regional Medical Center. She taught swimming, not singing, adopted one child, not two, and at times contacts healing guides, not healing gods.

THE INCORRECT
CORRECTIONS HALL OF FAME

- Our newspaper carried the notice last week that Mr. Oscar Hoffnagle is a defective on the police force. This was a typographical error. Mr. Hoffnagle is, of course, a detective on the police farce.

- Yesterday we mistakenly reported that a talk was given by a battle-scared hero. We apologize for the error. We obviously meant that the talk was given by a bottle-scarred hero.

- In a recent edition, we referred to the chairman of Chrysler Corporation as Lee Iacoocoo. His real name is Lee Iacacca. The *Gazette* regrets the error.

- The marriage of Miss Freda van Amburg and Willie Branton, which was announced in this paper a few weeks ago, was a mistake we wish to correct.

*Now is your chance to have your ears pierced
and get an extra pair to take home, too.*

Life's a Pitch

When you have had one of those "Take This Job and Shove It" days, try this: On your way home from work, stop at your pharmacy and go to the section where they have thermometers. You will need to purchase a rectal thermometer made by Q-Tip. Be very sure that you get this brand and this type of thermometer.

When you get home, lock your doors, draw the drapes, and disconnect the phone so you will not be disturbed during your therapy. Change to very comfortable clothing, such as a sweat suit, and lie down on your bed. Open the package and remove the thermometer. Carefully place it on the bedside table so that it will not become chipped or broken. Take out the written material that accompanies the thermometer and read it. You will notice in small print this statement:

"Every rectal thermometer made by Q-Tip is PERSONALLY tested."

Now, close your eyes and repeat out loud five times: "I am so glad I do not work in quality control at the Q-Tip company. I am so glad I do not work in quality control at the Q-Tip company. I am so glad . . . "

It's an ad, ad, ad, ad world we live in. Twenty years ago, the average person saw and heard about 800 advertising messages a day, through media including radio, television, newspapers, magazines, and billboards. Today the figure has climbed above 3,000 messages. Hundreds of thousands of ads compete for our attention and for the more than a trillion dollars—$1,000,000,000,000!—that Americans spend each year.

"The greatest sin in advertising," contends one expert, "is not to be noticed." You're about to read some ads that got noticed by me, your ever-vigilant anthologist, and a legion of other blooper snoopers. Our task has been aided by the happy truth that in some newspapers and magazines, the advertisements are more entertaining than the articles, stories, and special features.

The Latin phrase *caveat emptor* means "let the buyer beware." *Caveat lector:* let the reader beware of the claims made by the ads inflicted upon us in the print media:

- Now is your chance to have your ears pierced and get an extra pair to take home, too.
- Our vacuum cleaner sucks.
- Large mixing bowl wanted for woman with hard bottom and good for beating
- What a treat is in store for those who dine here. It is impossible to prepare a palatable meal for the price we ask.
- Don't break your back taking care of your lawn. Let us do it for you!
- If any piece proves defective, we will replace it with one of similar quality.
- Return this certificate to the Salvation Army with your Christmas gift and the reply form below to help provide Toys for Hurting Children.
- Sportswear Sale! Tops and bottoms. All half off.

- You can order our rings by post. State size or enclose a string tied around your finger.
- The hotel has bowling alleys, tennis courts, comfortable beds, and other athletic facilities.
- Have an immediate opening for a first-class stenographer, preferably one with some business sexperience
- Sears Convertible Free-Arm Sewing Machine
  Built-In Buttholer!
- All the chicken you can eat. This is the same delicious chicken we have been serving for the past five years.
- Valley Center Meat Market
  Low Low Prices. High Quality
  Happy Chanukah
  Whole Pork Loins $1.69 Lb.
- Saturday 10:00 A.M. Easter Matinee. Every child laying an egg in the doorman's hand will be admitted free. We want your eggs, and we want them bad.
- Not responsible from this date for any debts contracted by my wife. (Signed) J.A.S.
  He never did, why now?—(Signed) E.L.S.
- We offer competitive salaries, full benefits, and real growth opportunities that are often promised, but rarely delivered.
- Rebel Lube Service Center
  Free Earwash with Lube & Oil Change Only
- FOR SALE: Occasional chair by lady with carved clawed feet
- Lose all your weight for only $68.
- $100 Reward for information leading to the arrest and conviction of person who took wench from my Dodge Power Wagon
- Two female Boston Terrier puppies, seven wks. old. Perfect markings. Call 555-1234. Leave mess.
- PARKER—to the memory of George Parker, passed away September 10. Peace at last. From all the neighbors on his block.
- Divorce $99. Bankruptcy included.
- Sheer stockings. Designed for fancy dress, but so serviceable that lots of women wear nothing else.
- WANTED: Bedroom set for a girl in good condition.

- WANTED: Bartender, over 24, nondrinker, able to work staggered hours
- *In a Belfast newspaper:* WANTED: Man and woman to look after two cows, both Protestant
- HELP WANTED: Must have experience sewing, crafts, and quitting
- WANTED: Salesgirl. Must be respectable until after Christmas.
- WANTED: Man to wash dishes and two waitresses
- WANTED: Chambermaid in Rectory. Love in, $200 a month. References.
- WANTED: Sewer/manhole repair worker. Experienced only. Immediate opening.
- WANTED: Woman to hook rugs and a salesman
- WANTED: Used Paint
- Jack's Laundry.
  Leave your clothes here
  And spend the afternoon
  Having a good time.
- Snow Blower for Sale
  Only Used on Snowy Days
- '83 Toyota Hunchback—$2000
- Soft and genital bath tissue—89¢
- Shakespeare's Pizza—Free chopsticks
- Hummel's—Largest Selection Ever
  "If it's in stock, we have it!"
- Georgia Peaches—California Grown—89¢ lb.
- Nice parachutes—never opened—slightly stained
- LOST: Friday night, a small, red-faced lady's wristwatch; sentimental value
- Like new, 16-gauge shotgun for sale cheap. Also wedding dress and veil.
- Man with necessary equipment to spread manure
- Tired of working for only $9.75 per hour?
  We offer profit sharing and flexible hours.
  Starting pay: $7—$9 per hour.
- Joining nudist colony. Must sell washer & dryer. $300.
- Bar S sliced balogna—regular or tasty

- Lucy's floor covering & sofa selections. 12 moths interest-free.
- Open House
  Body Shapers Toning Salon
  Free coffee & donuts
- A hug selection of merchandise
- Free Soda (can)
  With Order of $10 or More
  Must mention coupon when ordering.
  No coupon necessary.
- Turkey smoked sausage. Beef added for better flavor.
- LOST: Male cat. Needs medication. Owner very worried, neutered, and declawed.
- TOPS (Take Off Pounds Sensibly) Meeting—5:30 VA Medical Center, overflow dining room
- FOR SALE: The personable belongings of Sharon Gallagher
- 20 percent off your first order of NI-712—the Natural Citrus Odor Eliminator
- Apt. for rent: Water, heat, garbage provided
- African Grey Parrot, tame and talking with cage
- Purebred miniature collie puppies. Tri-color and sable. Can see both parents.
- Dog training: Private and group class will teach your family and pet off-leash obedience.
- FOR SALE: Renault, 69,000 km, new tires, lady owner, always garaged
- The PTA is holding a rummage sale on Thursday. Please bring your rummage by Wednesday.
- *On a Tropicana Twisters drink bottle:* Flavors Mother Nature never intended
- Extra spacious one- and two-bedroom condominium homes featuring wall-to-wall windows
- Women having trouble getting pregnant are turning to Dr. Atherton.
- SEEKING SOMEONE SPECIAL: SWM seeks SF who is easygoing, sense of humor, who enjoys romantic evenings, life. Loves animals for friendship, possible relationship.
- 50 lb. potato—$6.00

- FOR SALE: An off-white girl's chest with drawers
- Vernon McLaren, Jr., PC
  Attorney at law
  10 percent Off Free Consultation
- Weekend Getaway: Enjoy the immunities at the Holiday Inn by the Bay.
  - Free: farm kittens, ready to eat
  - Jell-O brand toilet tissue, regular, sugar free, fat free
  - Main Street Pizza: We deliver, or pick up.

An ad appeared in the personals section of a city newspaper: "Professional man, 45, head on a stick, seeks similar woman." Investigation revealed that the ad writer had creatively reinterpreted what an advertiser had actually dictated, which was the word *hedonistic*.

The mother of all classified errors/audio errors may be this one from the San Diego *Union-Tribune*:

- I SEE YOU NURSE WANTED: RN with I See You experience or experienced RN willing to be trained in I See You techniques.

THE ADDLED ADS HALL OF FAME

- FOR SALE: Antique desk suitable for lady with thick legs and large drawers
- Tired of cleaning yourself? Let me do it.
- Our bikinis are exciting. They are simply the tops.
- Try our cough syrup. You will never get any better.
- WANTED: Young woman to pick fruit and produce at night
- FOR SALE: Pair Holstein oxen, 3200 lbs., eight years old, with horns capped by local blacksmith with brass balls

How's That Again?

He's a wolf in cheap clothing.

The Matron Saint of Word Botchers

There's one in every family and every office—the lovable relative, the high-and-mighty boss, or the clueless coworker who mangles the language malappropriately, the one who, when confronted with a choice between two words that sound alike, inevitably utters the wrong one.

"You've got to read these Buddisms," writes one devotee of *Anguished English*. Bud's the guy at work who keeps tripping on his own tongue and stepping on his syllables—the one who, without the slightest prevarication, tells his office mates, "No more negotiating—it's a dumb deal." Bud is a suppository of vagrant vocabulary. Bud yearns for a salary commiserate with his experience. Bud sees every crisis in the office as a potential disastrophe. Bud is clearly the employee most likely to become a wealthy typhoon. Watch out, or Bud will sue you for deformation of character.

Or there's Hazel, a favorite member of somebody's family who just wants a little piece of quiet. Naturally, her misspoken words are called Hazelisms. Hazel's the one who asks the waiter at the Chinese restaurant, "I'd like the chop suey, please. And hold the LSD." She's the one who telephones the family, "Come see me at the airport. We have a two-hour hangover." Hazel will likely tell you, "My cat Queenie has feline leukemia, and I may have to have it euphemized. If Queenie stops breathing, I'll give her VCR."

And Hazel is a veritable depository of information and of advice: "Don't ever wear yellow, dear. It makes your skin look shallow and emancipated." "When shipping fragile items, I always pack my box with xylophones." The points she makes are always mute—which I guess means they go without saying. She really knows how to get to the crust of the matter.

Malaproprisms are named after an "old weather-beaten she-dragon," Mrs. Malaprop, the comic centerpiece of Richard Brinsley Sheridan's 1775 play, *The Rivals*. Her name derives from *mal à propos*, which means "out of place, inappropriate." That's exactly what the words she uses are. In trying to impress others, particularly the wealthy Anthony Absolute, Mrs. Malaprop attempts to show off her inflated vocabulary.

The trouble is, the dowager doesn't know the meaning of big words. So she constantly confuses them with similar-sounding ones, inserting them into sentences in which they don't belong. She laments that "my affluence over my niece is very small" because the young woman is "as headstrong as an allegory [she meant 'alligator'] on the Nile." Still, the dowager urges her niece to "illiterate" (obliterate) an "illegible" (eligible) gentleman from her memory.

You might say that Mrs. Malaprop set out to be a bird-watcher, but ended up a word-botcher. What makes the situation especially humorous is that she is completely unaware of her verbal vagaries: "Sure, if I reprehend anything in this world, it is the use of my oracular tongue and a nice derangement of epitaphs." She meant, of course, that if she comprehended anything, it was the use of her oral tongue and a nice arrangement of epithets. Such errors illustrate the truth of Alexander Pope's pronouncement "a little knowledge is a dangerous thing":

In *The Daily Targum*, the student newspaper at Rutgers University, we read, "As soon as Jill Eikenberry, former *L.A. Law* star, discovered a lump on her breast in 1984, she knew it was cancer. . . . " So far, so good. But then: "The first doctor that Eikenberry consulted immediately recommended a radical vasectomy, the removal of the entire breast."

A flyer issued by an electric supply company in Philadelphia extolled the virtues of its health lounge chair vibrator kit: "Why not transform your ordinary reclining lounge or health chair into a really relaxing, enervating vibrating chair?" Nice try with that big word *enervating*. But the word means "weakening," exactly the opposite of what the ad writer thought.

A junior high school principal actually announced over the public address system, "Students must stop conjugating in the halls. This is inappropriate behavior." In mass defiance, the boys and girls roamed the halls intoning, "I am, you are, he is, we are, you are, they are."

Mrs. Malaprop first bestrode the stage more than two hundred years ago. But this grande dame of 18th-century comedy remains an aspiration to the erroneous, albeit euphonious, vocabulary that ricochets from our tongues and caroms off the roofs of our mouths:

- Pat Robertson and Jesse Jackson are diabolically opposed.
- He's a wolf in cheap clothing.
- Grandmother gave her air looms to the Hysterical Society.
- In the play, Lord Capulet sends out a servant to invite the guests. The servant couldn't read because he was illegitimate.
- The author puts women on a pedal stool.
- Who do you think you are, some kind of hexagon of virtue?
- Our son is 14 years old, but he is a very preconscious student.
- The chapter committees meet at the desecration of the committee chairman.
- During the last decade, the direction of Wolverine World seemed to hang in libido.
- We have to deal seriously with this serious offense as a detergent to others.

- I think this portfolio is a good example of my writing and an accurate betrayal of it.
- We have a new wienie dog. It's a datsun.
- Tonsorial operations are often performed with only a local anesthetic.
- I couldn't make it to class yesterday because I was sick, some kind of flu. There was nearly an academic in my fraternity house.
- My father died of a coronary conclusion.
- The Pope spoke to a large crowd during a beautification ceremony.
- The injury occurred to the gluttonous maximus.
- Living to be 100 isn't uncommon these days. City Clerk Joseph Shea said Quincy has 22 centurians.
- During the war the soldiers quickly built fornication out of buildings to hide in and shoot from.
- *On a college application:* I have a photogenic memory.
- When the Olympics were held here last year, lots of Cuban athletes deflected.
- The only sure-fire way to avoid teenage pregnancy is through obstenance.
- My wife can't get wired up because I can't find her erroneous zones.
- I always lend a synthetic ear to your problems.
- Her ex-husband received a decease and desist order.
- She digressed back to her childhood.
- Robert E. Lee abdicated the overthrow of the U.S. government.
- The sweat was coming off him in goblets.
- Her father was a civil serpent.
- Coworkers describe her as easy to work with and exhuming a great personality.
- He's a self-defecating person. That's why I admire him so much.
- I guess you're going to blame somebody, but you're not going to make a scrapegoat out of me.
- I'm going to have to cut down the walnut tree because it's infested with magnets.
- You know that local fire? They suspect arsenic.
- Solana Beach Nursery School seeking loving, neutering 2½-rear-old teacher. Beautiful work environment. Caring staff.

- Now it might get a little cool tonight, so just pull that African at the foot of the bed over you.
- Let's do this in one foul sweep.
- There are a lot of famous buildings in Italy, like the Leaning Tower of Pizza.
- Macy's is going to build a big store in Beverly Hills. It's going to be their starship.
- They live far away, out in the boondoggles.
- I exhilarated the engine, and the hood shot up.
- Please open the window. I'm getting sophisticated.
- Please, someone stop that incestuous pounding!
- Everything went all right, except my wife had to have a Sicilian section.
- We got it from a famous jazz musician, Felonius Monk.
- She'd been shut in so long, she had cabinet fever.
- I met this nice guy who's in the service. He's the chief petting officer.
- My mother is mean and short-tempered. I think she's going through her mental pause.
- We just had a plutonic friendship.
- I went to the library and looked it up on the micro fish.
- Please send this package via Partial Post.
- It takes two to tangle.
- They raised a great human cry.
- It was a case of love at Versailles.
- He's got one of those sight-seeing dogs.
- In Algiers, they spend most of their time at the cash bar.
- My sister has extra-century perception.
- A fool and his money are some party.
- All's fear in love and war.

These modern-day malaproprisms are not prefabrications. They are not pigments of the imagination. Rather, they were all actually uttered and recorded, plucked from the hum and buzz of real-life conversations and leaving us in a variable state of suspended admiration.

THE MALAPROPISTIC HALL OF FAME

- I don't want to cast asparagus at my opponent!
- Medieval cathedrals were supported by flying buttocks.
- Ortiz is the Sailors' most recent recipient of the pretentious Con Edison "Athlete of the Week."
- The mountain was named for the Reverend Starr King, who was an invertebrate climber and author of the book *The White Hills.*
- More and more people around the world are purchasing and using cellulite phones.
- I took up aerobics to help maintain my well-propositioned figure.

Gladly—the cross-eyed bear.

José, Can You See?

Two men were discussing Beatles songs. "I've never understood," one man wondered, "why they say, 'the girl with colitis goes by.'" After a puzzled pause, his friend lit up. "Ah," he said, "it's 'the girl with kaleidoscope eyes.' That's a line from 'Lucy in the Sky with Diamonds.'"

That's also a classic mondegreen.

What is a mondegreen? I'm glad I asked me that. A mondegreen is a mishearing of oft-used words, resulting in a misinterpretation of the lyrics of popular songs and hymns and the contents of patriotic affirmations, prayers, familiar adages and epigrams, advertising slogans, and the like.

Pop songs yield a bumper crop of mondegreens. "The girl from Emphysema goes walking" is a mondegreen for "the girl from Ipanima goes walking." "The ants are my friends" is a mondegreen for the first four words of "The answer, my friends, is blowin' in the wind."

"I've thrown a custard in her face" is not the national anthem for clowns. It's a mondegreen for "I've grown accustomed to her face," in *My Fair Lady*.

"Return December, bad dress unknown" is a mondegreen for "Return to sender, address unknown," and "Don't cry for me, Marge and Tina" a mondegreen for "Don't cry for me, Argentina."

To the surprise of many rock-and-roll enthusiasts, Jimi Hendrix sang, " 'Scuse me while I kiss the sky," not " 'Scuse me while I kiss this guy."

Actually, George Gershwin wrote *Rhapsody in Blue*, not *Rap City in Blue*.

"Clown control to Mao Zedong" is at least as colorful and imaginative as David Bowie's original lyric, "Ground control to Major Tom."

Herman's Hermits sang, "There's a kind of hush all over the world tonight," not "There's a can of fish all over the world tonight." But the fish are better.

And if Davy Crockett was "killed in a bar when he was only three," who was that at the Alamo?

The word *mondegreen* was coined by Sylvia Wright, who wrote a *Harper's* column about the phenomenon in 1954, in which she recounted hearing a Scottish folk ballad, "The Bonny Earl of Murray." She heard the lyric "Oh, they have slain the Earl of Murray/And Lady Mondegreen." Wright powerfully identified with Lady Mondegreen, the faithful friend of the Bonny Earl. Lady Mondegreen died for her liege with dignity and tragedy. How romantic!

It was some years later that Sylvia Wright learned that the last two lines of the stanza were really "Oh, they have slain the Earl of Murray/And laid him on the green." She named such sweet slips of the ear mondegreens, and thus they have been evermore.

Children are especially prone to fresh and unconventional interpretations of the boundaries that separate words. Our patriotic songs and statements have been delightfully revised by misspelt youth:

José, can you see
By the Donzerly light?
Oh, the ramrods we washed
Were so gallantly steaming.
And the rockets' red glare,
The bombs bursting in there,
Grapefruit through the night
That our flag was still rare.

◎

I pledge the pigeons to the flag
Of the United States of America
And to the republic for Richard Stans,
One naked individual, underground,
With liver, tea, injustice for all.

◎

God bless America, land that I love,
Stand aside, sir, and guide her,
With delight through the night from a bulb.

◎

America, America,
God's red Chef Boyardee.

◎

Miniza seen the glory
Of the coming of the Lord.
He has trampled out the vintage
Where the great giraffes are stored.

And it's "Oh, beautiful for spacious skies," not "Oh, beautiful for space ship guys."

Another territory lush with mondegreens is religion. Many a youngster has recited the famous line from the 23rd Psalm as "Shirley, good Mrs. Murphy will follow me all the days of my life." Many other imaginary characters inhabit the lyrics of hymns and words from the Bible. Battalions of children have grown up singing about an opthalmalogically challenged ursine named Gladly—"the cross-eyed bear."

> *Our Father, Art, in heaven, Harold be Thy name.*
> *Thy King done come, Thy will be done,*
> *On earth as it is in heaven.*
> *Give us this day our jelly bread,*
> *And forgive us our press passes,*
> *As we forgive those who press past us.*
> *And lead us not into Penn Station,*
> *But deliver us some e-mail.*

For religious mondegreens, the fracturing of Christmas carols especially opens up new worlds of meaning and imagination. Try singing along with these new takes on old favorites, revised by children:

- *Good King Wences' car backed out*
  On a piece of Stephen.
- *Deck the halls with Buddy Holly.*
- *We three kings of porridge and tar*
- *On the first day of Christmas my tulip gave to me*
- *Later on we'll perspire, as we dream by the fire.*
- *He's making a list, of chicken and rice.*
- *Noel, Noel, Barney's the king of Israel.*
- *Bells on bobtail ring,*
  Making spareribs bright.
- *Get a yuck, get a yuck, get a yuck yuck yuck.*
- *With the jelly toast proclaim*
- *Olive, the other reindeer*
- *You'll go down in Listerine.*
- *Frosty the Snowman is a ferret elf, I say.*
- *In the meadow we can build a snowman,*
  Then pretend that he is sparse and brown.
- *Sleep in heavenly peas, sleep in heavenly peas.*
- *Chipmunks roasting on an open fire*
- *Oh, what fun it is to ride with one horse, soap, and hay.*

- *O come, froggy faithful.*
- *What a friend we have in cheeses.*
- *You'll tell Carol, "Be a skunk, I require."*
- *Where shepherds washed their socks by night*
- *Get dressed, ye married gentlemen, get huffing you this May.*
- *Round John Virgin, mother and child,*
  Holy Vincent, so tender and mild

I nominate Richard Stans, Art, Harold, good Mrs. Shirley Murphy, Round John Virgin, Vincent, a reindeer named Olive, and that cross-eyed bear named Gladly for a pullet surprise. But the ultimate winner, who received her prize posthumorously, of course, must be . . . Lady Mondegreen!

THE MONDEGREEN HALL OF FAME

The mondegreening of America can be seen and heard in language outside of songs, prayers, adages, and slogans:

- Maggie was the valid victorian of our class.
- Blacks are especially prone to suffer from sick as hell anemia.
- Proteins are composed of a mean old acid.
- With youth in Asia being a big question of right or wrong in today's society, hospitals fear that they will be sued.
- Taking this course will raise our essay tee scores. Higher essay tee scores are always a good thing.
- Spice up your omelet by adding some hollow penis.
- In separate submissions, twin sisters described a serial killer as a cycle path and a lunar dick.

That cat sure is a strange duck.

Metaphors Be
with You

Much as I hate to stick my neck out on a limb and chew your ear, I'm as happy as a pig in a poke to exhibit a chapter on mixed-up metaphors—figures of speech that are guaranteed to kindle a flood of laughter in you. It's time to swallow the bullet, fish or get off the pot, and take the bull by the tail and look it in the eye.

I don't want to stir up sleeping dogs and I don't want to open a fine kettle of worms, but I've got a mind like a steel sieve. So I know how much people love to make metaphors—figures of speech that contain fanciful comparisons. But when metaphors collide, the produce a horse of a different feather. Sometimes those metaphors become albatrosses on our backs or monkeys around our necks. Then we feel caught between a rock and the deep blue sea and up the creek without a pot to pee in. We find that skating on thin ice gets us into hot water. But that's all spilt milk under the bridge.

When the tongue trips lightly and hurriedly ahead of the speech figure formed in a busy and cluttered mind, the speaker can end up barking up the wrong pew, burning the midnight candle, and grasping at straws to drive home his or her point. The resulting mixed-up metaphors are worth their weight in salt. Finding these exquisitely mixed-up metaphors is like pulling hens' teeth. That's the whole kettle of fish in a nutshell.

I have bent over out of my way to ensure that the metaphors above are all real, genuine, certified, and authentic. And most are malaphors—two metaphoric clichés that have been joked together kicking and screaming. "Stick my neck out" and "going out on a limb" become melded into "stick my neck out on a limb." "Worth their weight in gold" and "worth their salt" get telescoped into "worth their weight in salt." "Deaf as a post" and "dead as a doornail" get run through the language blender and come out as "deaf as a doornail." That's how language can pull the wool right out from under our feet in midstream.

In a fund-raising letter by Bob Dole, candidate for U.S. president: "To win, we must not only match the liberal Democrats' intensity. We must be even more determined to bring our nation the long needed change its people have been crying out for. You can decide our fate. Do we put our shoulder to the grindstone and move forward, or do we let up and hope momentum can carry our candidates to victory?"

Mr. Dole lost that election and went on to become a spokesman for Viagra, making Americans aware of the term "erectile dysfunction." That dysfunction may have been complicated by his putting his shoulder to the grindstone.

The same grindstone does its work in a statement uttered by James B. McSheehy, longtime member of the San Francisco Board of Supervisors: "Gentlemen, when the chickens come home to roost, the shoe may be on the other foot, for you can't drive the ship of state down the middle of the road and still keep your nose to the grindstone."

Pop culture icon Cher can mangle a metaphor with the best of them: "I've been up and down so many times that I feel as if I'm in a revolving door." Even more of a metaphor melder was bandleader Lawrence Welk, who gave the world such gems as "the way you play that suits me like a glove" and "my records today are selling like wild cakes."

Once speakers have created such Siamese metaphors, they have buttered their bread, and now they have to sleep in it. Or as Walter Rogers, member of Congress from Texas, proclaimed, "If we don't stop shearing the wool off the sheep that lays the golden egg, we'll pump it dry."

It's no skin off my teeth, so here, off the cuff of my head, are some figures of speech that just don't figure:

• You're trying to make this a hurricane in a Teapot Dome and making a mountain out of a mole hole.

• They're putting the chicken before the cart.

• Today there are some among us who are willing to knock down the ladder of opportunity after they themselves have reached the top rung.

• The O.J. news might be over, its effervescence draining downward in a great sucking sound of tumbling talking heads.

• Cystitis is a living death, it really is. Nobody ever talks about it, but if I was faced with a choice between having my arms removed and getting cyctitis, I'd wave good-bye to my arms happily.

• That cat sure is a strange duck.

• Spooks were clucking their tongues at the ham-handed gumshoes.

• There will be little appetite for ratcheting up the stakes if this is for the long haul.

• Edy's opinion of the latest Häagen-Dazs flavor: It's nothing to rave home about.

• Dave, a hard-driving 50-year-old vice president, had one coronary under his belt and another on the way when he decided to opt out of corporate work.

• All this will enable Hong Kong to stamp its mark on the world stage.

• The playwright has taken material as stale as yesterday's bagel and woven it into a phantasmagorical comedy of both lacerating humor and infinite compassion.

• What that woman did was blow me off my feet.

• Roberts has almost caught Jones. He's breathing down his throat.

• A loose tongue spoils the whole broth.

- We wouldn't eat it with a ten-foot pole.
- It's either fame or famine.
- I came out of that deal smelling like a bandit.
- Whenever businesses find themselves in uncharted waters, they tend to stick their heads in the sand.
- I'm going to sit on the back burner for a while.
- He's been a sore thumb in my side.
- I know your game like the back of a book.
- He's not the one with his ass in a noose.
- We put all our heads together and shot from the hip.
- The newsletter, called *Flashpoint,* is a kind of freewheeling smorgasbord of conspiracy theories, as mesmerizing as a hypnotist's watch.
- I shot the wind out of his saddle.
- As easy as taking candy from a drowning man.
- At least we're not standing around on our thumbs.
- Take the bull and run with it.
- The limo rental business is not a good one. It's a stop-and-go business.
- You must turn the other eye.
- Don't have a gasket.
- Take a flying hike.
- It's all moth-eared.
- I want to hear it so quiet we can hear a mouse dropping.
- I won't sit on a keg of nails not knowing where I stand.
- He's on shaky ground, like a cat on a tin roof in a rainstorm.
- I'm afraid he already bit the farm.
- There's more than one way to skin a goose.
- Coffee isn't my cup of tea.

THE MIXED-UP METAPHORS HALL OF FAME

- During the Napoleonic era, the crowned heads of Europe were trembling in their shoes.

  —high school student blooper

- The communist menace is a snake in the grass that is gnawing away at the foundation of the ship of state.

  —in a University of Chicago student essay

- The poet Dante stood with one foot firmly planted in the Middle Ages while with the other he saluted the rising dawn of the Renaissance.

  —in a Brown University student essay

- You're biting the hand of the goose that laid the golden egg.

  —Samuel Goldwyn

- I wish my butt did not go sideways, but I guess I have to face that.

  —Christie Brinkley

- It has been our purpose all along to have sort of a periodical potpourri to cover all this flotsam and jetsam that flies through the media that can get nailed down on a regular, periodic track. So, in a sense, that can be interpreted as open sesame, but don't throw darts.

  —Chicago mayor Harold Washington

After-
Christmas
Sale!
Starts Today–
December 21!

Hodge Podge Logic

During the 1994 Miss USA beauty pageant, Miss Alabama was asked, "If you could live forever, would you and why?" Her answer: "I would not live forever, because we should not live forever, because if we were supposed to live forever, then we would live forever, but we cannot live forever, which is why I would not live forever."

Reported a Knight Ridder News Service dispatch, "The crime bill passed by the senate would reinstate the federal death penalty for certain violent crimes: assassinating the President; hijacking an airliner; and murdering a government poultry inspector."

"Beginning in February 1976 your assistance benefits will be discontinued. Reason: It has been reported to our office that you expired on January 1, 1976," explained a letter from the Illinois Department of Public Aid.

"When I told the people of Northern Ireland that I was an atheist," related Quentin Crisp, "a woman in the audience stood up and asked, 'Yes, but is it the God of the Catholics or the God of the Protestants in whom you don't believe?'"

A broadcast report noted that the "Supreme Court is reviewing a request by prisons to allow use of a new drug developed for lethal injections, even though it has not been certified safe and effective by the Food and Drug Administration."

Convicted murderer William "Cody" Neal asserted at his sentencing hearing, "I accept responsibility for the murder. If I lose my life, I can live with that."

And, a Pratt & Whitney spokesperson explained why the company charged the Air Force nearly $1,000 for an ordinary pair of pliers: "They're multipurpose. Not only do they put the clips on, but they take them off."

English is a language not noted for its logic. If adults commit adultery, do infants commit infantry? If olive oil is made from olives, what do they make baby oil from? If a vegetarian eats vegetables, what does a humanitarian consume? And if *pro* and *con* are opposites, is *progress* the opposite of *congress*?

No wonder then that our glorious, uproarious English language can at times appear to be a bubble off plumb, a sandwich short of a picnic, and two french fries short of a Happy Meal:

• I married a few people I shouldn't have, but haven't we all?—*Mamie Van Doren*
• I'll never make the mistake of turning 70 again.—*Casey Stengel*
• Same-Day Dry Cleaning—All Garments Ready in 48 Hours
• I make it a rule never to eat on an empty stomach.
• There's nothing that weighs more per ounce than *National Geographic*.
• Homeless people are younger and more often than the general population.
• Two-dimensional photographs don't do this car justice.
• Don't go into darkened parking lots unless they are well lighted.

- Suits $195–$245 (regular $136.50–$171.50)
  Sport Coats $100–$145 (regular $70–$101.50)
  Dress Slacks $38–$50 (regular $26.50–$35)
- *In a gas station:* Cokes $.49/2 for $1
- *In a group insurance handbook:* If your medical insurance terminates for any reason including death, you may elect within 30 days to continue such medical insurance.
- Please Type or Print Legibly.
- A little pain never hurt anyone.
- Shakespeare couldn't have a favorite actress. They didn't have women during Shakespeare's time.
- *On a leaflet:* If you cannot read, this leaflet will tell you how to get lessons.
- Fifty-five percent of young people looking for their first jobs are unemployed.
- Serious crime in the county dipped slightly in the first half of the year, but rape, robbery, theft, and homicides posted increases.
- Stanley Kubrick's absence will certainly be missed at the film's premiere.
- This event should not go unforgotten.
- New drugs may contain AIDS, but not all can afford them.
- Doctor Swears Under Oath
  California Housewife
  Lost 12 lbs. In 7 Days
  Using Amazing New
  "ONE DAY DIET"
- It's pronounced just like it sounds.
- As you will see, the limitations of this product are endless.
- They're going to like it whether they like it or not.
- Things never seem as they appear to be.
- Come to think about it, I hadn't thought about it.
- You can get two free drinks for the price of one.
- Buy one dozen free and get another half dozen.
- We larger people have to wear darker sizes.
- *In a National Public Radio interview on kosher slaughtering:* Killing an animal while it is still alive is unacceptable.

- Once he'd gone past the point of no return, there was no going back.
- Publicize your business absolutely free. Send $6.
- The only difference between me and a madman is that I am not mad.—*Salvador Dali*
- *In a Dear Abby column:* It is normal for survivors of suicide to experience feelings of guilt.
- Turn your coins into cash today.
- *Ad for answering machine:* You may leave messages of any length up to five minutes.
- China is a big country, inhabited by many Chinese.—*French president Charles de Gaulle*
- Charles Whiteside had suffered from attacks of pneumonia and jaundice, but he died from arterial sclerosis. "It will be a miracle if he ever paints again," said his wife Allison.
- Nobody is consistent consistently.
- Normally, she's pretty normal.
- I think I have an incredible level of credibility.
- I think it's important that the store was founded in 1898 and is still in existence with the same name and customers.
- For some context, consider these numbers from the same year: 91 percent of clergy were men, 92 percent of engineers were men, and 90 percent of men were dentists.
- Last night in the NBA, most of the winning teams that played won.
- My uncle Bertie, who lives in London, has said that a London fog can get so thick that you can't see what the bloody weather is like!
- There are good days and there are bad days, and this is one of them.—*Lawrence Welk*
- *Weather forecast by a TV station:* Severe thunderstorm watch until 4:30 this afternoon. Stay inside. Do not use electrical appliances. Please stay tuned for further information.
- Late one morning, discussing why the cleaning lady hasn't shown up, Edy says, "She's never this late unless she isn't coming."
- If you can't keep quiet, shut up!
- Go see for yourself why you shouldn't see that film.
- All generalizations are bad.

- He made a left turn into a wrong-way street.
- She's the same age I am, but a year older.
- 24-Hour Money Center

    L.A. ATM: Hours of Operation: 6 A.M. until 6 P.M., seven days a week

    Almost Open 24 Hours
- Tell the client that the campaign we've created is doomed to success.
- Every single man in that room was married.

THE ILLOGICAL
LOGIC HALL OF FAME

- *On an airplane:* If you are sitting in an exit row and you cannot read this card or cannot see well enough to follow these instructions, please tell a crew member.
- I don't care if my movie makes a cent. I just want every man, woman, and child in America to see it.—*Samuel Goldwyn*
- Thank God I'm still an atheist.—*Salvador Dali*
- *On the bombing of a Vietnamese village:* We had to destroy that town in order to save it.
- Nobody comes here—it's too crowded.—*Yogi Berra*
- Recent tests conducted by a zoologist prove that grasshoppers hear with their legs. In all cases, the insects hopped when a tuning fork was sounded nearby. There was no reaction to this stimulus, however, when the insects' legs had been removed.

Give half teaspoon four times daily for funny nose.

Loopy Labels

The following instructions have appeared on some U.S. Navy warheads: "It is necessary for technical reasons that these warheads should be stored with the top at the bottom and the bottom at the top. In order that there may be no doubt as to which is the top and which is the bottom, for storage purposes it will be seen that the bottom of each head has been labeled with the word TOP."

On the pages of an instruction manual for masons and bricklayers appeared this helpful hint: "Be careful not to lay the bricks so close apart. Place them farther together." Somebody threw up a brick with that one.

Those are just two topsy-turvy examples of misdirected directions.

Here is a lineup of loopy labeling logic and penetrating glimpses into the obvious on the products that line our supermarket shelves:

- *On a Sears hairdryer:* Do not use while sleeping.
- *On a bag of Fritos:* You could be a winner! No purchase necessary. Details inside.
- *On a bar of Dial soap:* Directions: Use like regular soap.
- *In a prescription for a child:* Give half teaspoon four times daily for funny nose.
- *On a frozen dinner box:* Serving suggestion: Defrost.
- *On a Zippo lighter:* Do not ignite in face.
- *On a hotel-provided shower cap in a box:* Fits one head.
- *On the bottom of a Tesco's Tirimasu dessert:* Do not turn upside down.
- *On packaging for a Rowenta iron:* Do not iron clothes on body.
- *On a dessert package:* This packet of ready-made pastry will make enough for four persons or 12 tarts.
- *On a package of Top Cog fan belts:* Do not change the belt while the engine is running.
- *On Boots Children's cough medicine:* Do not drive car or operate machinery.
- *On a Pop-Tart box:* Warning—Filling may be hot when heated.
- *On a packet of Nytol sleeping aids:* Warning—may cause drowsiness.
- *On Manischewitz Instant Potato Soup, which comes in its own Styrofoam cup:* Fill to the rim with boiling water. Stir vigorously.
- *On a string of Christmas lights made in China:* For indoor or outdoor use only.
- *On a candle:* Caution—may be flammable.
- *On a Japanese food processor:* Not to be used for the other use.
- *On Saintsbury's PEANUTS:* Warning—contains nuts.
- *On a Swedish chainsaw:* Do not attempt to stop chain with your hands.
- *On a credit card sleeve:* Please use this sleeve to protect the magnetic strip on your Bell Atlantic Credit Card from Chase.
- *On a clothing label:* Machine wash cold, gentle cycle, tumble dry low. Torch up with iron, if necessary.

- *On the "CycleAware" helmet-mounted mirror:* Remember: Objects in the mirror are actually behind you.
- *On a car lock that loops around both the clutch pedal and the steering wheel:* Warning—remove lock before driving.
- *On a packet of juggling balls:* This product contains small granules under three millimeters. Not suitable for children under the age of 14 years in Europe or 8 years in the USA.
- *On a packet of peanuts served on an internal flight in China (written in both English and Chinese):* Open packet and eat contents.
- *On a camera:* This camera only works when there is film inside.
- *On a bottle of flavored milk drink:* After opening, keep upright.
- *On a can of insect spray:* Kills all kinds of insects! Warning—this spray is harmful to bees.
- *On another brand of insect spray:* Kills flies, wasps, mosquitoes, midges, and other flying insects. Not tested on animals.
- *On a box of Band-Aids:* For medical emergencies seek professional help.
- *On an aspirin bottle:* Do not use product if bottle is opened.
- *On an ocean buoy for determining the position of submarines:* Protect from seawater.
- *In a brochure for Healthometer EVERWeigh bathroom scales:* The capacity of the scale is 330 pounds. To prevent damage, do not try to weigh more than 330 pounds.
- *On a large folding cardboard sunshade for car windscreens:* Do not attempt to operate vehicle with sunshade in place.
- *On another sun shield label:* May fade in direct sunlight.
- *On a can of windscreen de-icing spray:* Spray works in freezing temperatures.
- *On a Halloween Batman costume:* This cape does not give the wearer the ability to fly.
- *On a pair of jeans:* Wash and dry separately.
- *On a package of cake:* Pineapple upside downs. Stand on head. Then eat.
- *On a bathroom scale:* Permanently adjusted.
- *On bottles of Rave shampoo:* To unclog pump, run under warm water.
- *From the Indigo PC Owners' Manual:* Hardware dos and don'ts: Do not dangle the mouse by its cable or throw mouse at coworkers.

- *On a box of Toilet Duck bowl cleaner tablets:* Bowl water is not harmful to children or pets. However, as standard practice, it is not recommended that pets drink water from the toilet.
- *On the bottom of a wind-up kitchen timer:* Do not place on or near heat-producing appliances.
- *From a manual on a vehicle with extendable mast:* Warning:—Do not climb mast when erect.
- *Inside a box of a "Kool Tie":* Hand rinse in a product that contains no phosphates and is biodegradable for no more than three minutes.
- *On a stir fry pan:* Do not use mental tools for prolonging the life of the pan.
- *On a paper-towel dispenser:* Pull down. Tear up.
- *On a restroom paper-towel dispenser:* If no paper, use manual feed wheel.
- *On a box of rest-room towel rollers:* Warning! Improper use may cause injury or death!

THE BRAND-NEW BLOOPERS HALL OF FAME

- In Spanish, the "Nova" in Chevy Nova is "no va"—"It doesn't go."
- The Chinese characters chosen to represent Coca-Cola translate into "bite the wax tadpole."
- In German, the Rolls-Royce Silver Mist and Clairol's Mist Stick mean "human waste."
- In some Latin countries, Parker's Jotter pens signify "jockstrap."
- In Tagalog, the major dialect group in the Phillipines, the first two syllables of Viagra mean "scrotum."
- . . . and can anybody explain why Kiwi International Airlines is named after a bird that can't fly?

Grammar
Gremlins

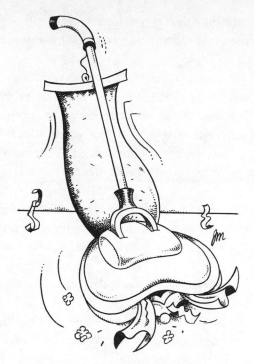

Give an example of a collective noun.
Vacuum cleaner.

What's Wrong with This Picture?

Many children's magazines feature puzzles in which the young readers are asked to "find what's wrong with this picture." Typically, a pitcher is missing a handle or a table a leg or a clock a hand. Shoes and socks are mismated, a tiger sports a mane, a picture hangs akimbo or upside down. There's a similar challenge we get when we have to slog our way through a carelessly constructed sentence. Parts are missing, parts don't match, parts are the wrong size, parts don't work together. Now return to those thrilling days of yesteryear and try to see what's wrong with each of these prose pictures, each created by surreal syntax:

• The *Northern Star,* the student newspaper of our university, has an opening for a proofer. The job requires grammatical proficiency, an eye for design, and are available to work afternoons and evenings.

• English First, the organization that would like to have English made the official language of the United States, sent out a letter that included this grammatically challenged sentence: "Now it is up to you and I to convince them."

• After a 12-year courtship, Greenspan and NBC news correspondent Andrea Mitchell were married by Supreme Court Justice Ruth Bader Ginsburg in April. They live in her house near the Chain Bridge in Washington.

• Hooters is known for its skimpily clad waitresses and chicken wings.

• Discovered at 5:06 P.M., the flames spread so rapidly that the first firemen on the scene were driven back to safety and leaped across three streets to ignite other buildings.

• He had apparently bounced on the track and suffered a small cut on the head, which needed three stitches, and some bruises.

• When the baby is done drinking, it must be unscrewed and laid in a cool place under the tap. If the baby does not thrive on fresh milk, it should be boiled.

• Admiral Peary's daughter wrote that, if Peary's father had not died when he was two years old, the chances are that Peary would have entered the family lumber business instead of becoming an Arctic explorer.

• The department has been careful to ensure that enumerators will stand out and be easily recognized. All of them will wear specially laminated badges that must be signed by the director of statistics and a special fluorescent vest.

• For anyone who has children and doesn't know it, there is a day care on the first floor.

• Two new booklets are available for South Carolinians who are survivors of head injuries and their families.

• Newspaper have a lot to worry about.

- The Writer's Forum: Do you enjoy writing and are looking for helpful criticism to improve?

- Tadashi Osaka said he planned to provide Thai students with easy-to-understand picture books and learned Japanese airlines dispose of picture books for children when they get old.

- Jodi almost didn't get to go on the Washington trip because she had to have major surgery on her ear—the eighth one—in February.

- *Posted in an exhibit at the* Titanic *Museum in Indian Orchard, Massachusetts:* These postcards were donated by Helen Huber, on behalf of her great-uncle, Gerhard Huber, who perished in the *Titanic* disaster and had been in a steamer trunk for 30 years.

- The woman was searched by border guards using drug-sniffing dogs and her car.

- Mr. Cram lives with his wife, his high school sweetheart, and three sons.

- Alan Henderson has battled weak ankles, now made stronger by exercise, assorted muscle pulls, and a prolonged bout with pancreatitis.

- When washing windows, add a small quantity of vinegar to the water. This will keep flies away as well as cleaning them.

- One morning, I sent Ruby, my cat, into the bathroom to work out his problems and shut the door.

- Clinton's father died shortly before his birth.

- I wish we had never put a police officer in a school or metal detector.

- A city circuit court has awarded $3.5 million to a retired Bethlehem Steel worker who was exposed to asbestos and his wife.

During a grammar class, the teacher asked her students to "Give me an example of a double negative."

"Never-Never Land," offered one of the students.

"No, that's not a double negative," said the teacher.

"I don't know no double negatives," sighed the student.

Written quizzes about grammar have elicited equally bizarre grammar stammers:

What is grammar?

Grammar is my mother's mother.

What are the parts of speech?

The parts of speech are lungs and air.

What is a pronoun?

A pronoun is a professional noun.

What is syntax?

Syntax is all the money collected at the church from sinners.

Give an example of a collective noun.

Vacuum cleaner.

THE UNGRAMMATICAL HALL OF FAME

- Statewide, students performed extremely poor on the writing section of the exam.
- Old Sedbergians are invited to a weekend reunion at the school. We would like to extend a particularly warm invitation to all of you who left Sedbergh and your wives.
- The easiest hole on the course, Deb Richards found the fairway bunker both times she played it.
- Females should have the same athletic opportunities as males. It is an almost universal medical opinion that there is no sport more dangerous to a girl than a boy.
- I had an infection after the operation and was on antibiotics for two weeks. There were still some minor pains in my testicles, but they disappeared.

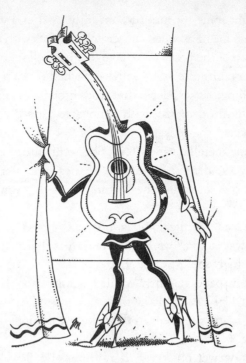

"Jewel has certainly made her mark by being perhaps the first folksinger to regularly take the stage with her guitar in four-inch heels and a miniskirt."

Stamp Out Flying Modifiers

A young law school graduate was interviewing with a judge for a clerkship. After carefully studying the young man's application, the judge asked, "Do you understand you have a dangling participle?" The young man jumped up and yelled, "Get it off me!"

Dangling participles and misplaced modifiers aren't insects that cling to our clothing. But they beat their wings around our statements, infest our sentences, and chomp away at intelligibility. They're the peculiar juxtapositions that defy grammar but generate humor:

"We bought some cat furniture recently," writes a woman in New England, "which means wooden cat scratching posts with carpet-covered platforms on top of the posts. (We have four cats, all indoor, and a lot of shredded human furniture as a result.) Attached to each and every one of these scratching posts is a label that reads proudly in large bold letters, 'Real wooden furniture for cats with removable parts.' "

"Not our cats," she adds.

When some metallic ear writes, "She went into the hospital after being bitten by a spider in a bathing suit," we scratch our heads and ask ourselves, "Who was wearing the bathing suit—the woman or the spider?"

When we read, "While doing laundry, a Cabot House student's laptop computer was stolen," we remind ourselves that computers are becoming increasingly sophisticated, but . . .

When a newspaper reports, "While jogging across the Curve Street Bridge at about 11:10 A.M., a large BFI truck crossed the bridge at a high rate of speed, forcing a resident to the side," we conjure up the image of a jogging truck.

When a reviewer observes, "If nothing else, Jewel has certainly made her mark by being perhaps the first folksinger to regularly take the stage with her guitar in four-inch heels and a miniskirt," we wryly comment, "I'll bet that the guitar will steal the show!"

That's the problem with mislocated modifiers. They leave us firmly planted on midair. They spin the brain into images of a surreal world. They cry havoc and let slip the dogs of confusion.

Even a single word misplaced can wreak havoc on a sentence and thought. Note the especially misplaced modifier "especially" in the letter from the president of a charitable organization: "I am especially appealing to those of you who do not usually attend fund-raising events."

And note, too, the lead story in an issue of The Appalachian, the college newspaper of Appalachian State University, in Boone, North Carolina. The headline blared, ACADEMIC INTEGRITY CODE TO BE REVISED.

The opening sentence announced, "Outdated and long-winded, the Appalachian State University Academic Integrity Committee has been charged with the task of revising the current Academic Integrity Code."

One paragraph later in the same article, the reader was informed,

"Last revised in December 1989, the committee was designed to create a current code and implement honor codes for students to follow."

Was the committee outdated, long-winded, and last revised in December 1989? Maybe so, but we can assume that the paper didn't wish to broadcast that opinion.

Sometimes the two-headedness of a two-headed headline rears its ugly heads because, even within the small space allotted, a modifier has been misplaced:

NINE DAYS AFTER DEATH,
NIXON APPLAUDS SINGER

◎

SATELLITE TRACKS COWS FROM OUTER SPACE

◎

SEALS DETECT FISH WITH WHISKERS

◎

TEEN IS STRUCK BY CAR TRYING TO CATCH BALL

◎

DEER INTERFERING WITH JETS
BEING SHOT AT PHILLY AIRPORT

◎

TICK-BORNE ILLNESS
KNOWN TO AFFECT DOGS
FOUND IN HUMANS

What do the following wayward modifiers have in common?:

• Larson, who drives a 1989 Honda Accord, was convicted of driving while intoxicated in the New London District Court in May 1994.
• Nathan Koenig, 19, of Riverside, was arrested for illegal consumption of alcohol by Monmouth police Saturday at 11:14 P.M.
• A six-year-old boy was found handcuffed to a bed by policemen.

- The cause of the blaze has been determined to be arson by Sheriff Detective Ronald Walker.
- Bernard Masling, of Lansburg, was charged with a felony count of second-degree sexual assault with an unconscious person during an appearance in Eau Claire County Circuit Court.
- The marriage was annulled in December 1969 on the grounds of adultery in the Philadelphia County Court.

Do these statements offer evidence that the police and the courts are corrupt? No. Each sentence is afflicted with a straying or unattached delinquent modifier. It is truly amazing how many people dangle their participles in public and never get arrested:

- The Nebraska legislature was asked to enact a law providing annulment of marriages of all couples who do not within three years after the wedding have one or more children by Representative Mangan, Democrat of Omaha, who is a bachelor.
- Tim West has written eight short plays produced in San Diego. The first of these was *Two Minutes*, a series of original comedic monologues for women mounted at St. Cecelia's for the annual Actors Festival.
- Former husband Alex Dudko and his daughter learned of "Red" Lucy's desperate mission to rescue her lover from the television news.
- The Diamondbacks' starter was facing a man who can knock any pitch he can reach over the fence.
- Power forward Dennis Rodman was suspended for a low blow by the NBA.
- The store clerk brought beer to the girls, who were waiting outside, in a plastic bag.
- A clean-shaven Robert Downey, Jr., who walked into court wearing an orange jail jumpsuit with slicked-back hair, told the judge he understood why the court's patience had run out.
- Subject still attends the Methodist Church, where he was married regularly.
- FOR SALE: A cross-cut saw by a Lyndon man with newly sharpened teeth
- The women in our country have legally had the right to choose abortion if pregnant for 26 years.

- They delivered 66 food packages to the elderly residents living locally in a large box.
- Three floors tall, the contractor began work on the upper level and worked his way down.
- National Public Radio has been working to make economics understandable for 50 years.
- The cause of death was determined to be strangulation by the medical examiner.
- The natives produce all manner of curios, the great majority of which appear to command a ready sale among visitors, crude and commonplace as these frequently are.
- I whispered a suggestion that we take a walk into her ear.
- You probably got a letter warning you about the dangers of lead-contaminated water in your mail.
- The mother of the accused railway murderer said that God would judge her son in a news conference on Friday.
- When my husband died, on the advice of my lawyer, I deeded my home to my two children.
- This is Red Ribbon Week. Students are asked to pledge to be drug free this week at lunch.
- One longtime resident recalled the days when Manhattan borough president Mary Slocumb used to stroll around the neighborhood gathering signatures in long skirts.
- American Catholic theologians will have to wait and see the exact wording of a French document permitting the use of condoms before engaging in theological debate.
- Tagament is now available without a prescription for heartburn.
- Dense and fruity, you'll find this reminiscent of holiday fruitcakes from the past.—*Weight Watchers Complete Cookbook*
- Prince Charles admitted committing adultery on television back in 1994.
- Employees requesting safety shoe reimbursement, limited to one pair per year, must complete and submit an expense account form, attaching proof of purchase to their supervisor.
- You can see many exquisite statues walking around the museum.
- Free brochure on childhood accidents in English and Spanish
- Mrs. Donahue found the cat using our lost-and-found column.

- Mrs. Jensen is reported to be resting comfortably by her doctor.
- His trouble stemmed from the fact that his glasses were thicker than an old Coke bottle and he was in an apartment brightened by a 60-watt bulb armed only with an eighth-grade education.
- Under the old policy, the superintendent was informed that a student was infected by the Department of Public Education.
- Mrs. Clinton said she found it "profoundly sad" that rumors circulated about her relationship with Vincent Foster after his suicide last summer.
- This is a charming, colonial hotel for tourists counting their pennies on the beach with laid-back staff and simple facilities.
- The bride was given in marriage by her father, wearing her mother's wedding gown.
- U.S. District Court order forced the Transit Authority to permit advertisements promoting the use of condoms on trains.
- We saw lots of squirrels going to and from church.
- Legally blind, doctors had told her recently that soon her sight would be entirely gone.
- Oxana Biyul talks about the drunk driving arrest that nearly ended her career here on *Entertainment Tonight*.
- LOST: A walking stick by an elderly man with a curiously carved ivory head
- Before you make a decision, please discuss the idea of a day at the beach with your physician.
- Born Herman Tobatchnakoff in St. Louis, at the age of four, he, his brother, and mother were left penniless when his father deserted the family.
- A North Clarendon woman will undergo a psychiatric evaluation after she threatened to shoot three Vermont State Police troopers tomorrow.
- The poet showed up with socks up to his knees that didn't match.

THE MISPLACED MODIFIERS
HALL OF FAME

- (1987) Yoko Ono will talk about her husband John Lennon, who was killed in an interview with Barbara Walters.
- (1993) Former hostage Terry Anderson talks about his five years of confinement in Beirut with Barbara Walters in a specially expanded segment of *20/20* at 10 on Channel Five.
- (1996) The diving and amateur sports community was in shock Thursday following disclosure by Olympic diver Greg Louganis, who speaks freely of his contracting AIDS in a *20/20* interview with Barbara Walters to be broadcast on ABC tonight.

My father received a letter by special devilry.

Laffing at
Missed Aches

A man, wanting to rob a downtown Corpus Christi Bank of America, walked into the branch and wrote, "This iz a stikkup. Put all your muny in this bag."

While standing in line, waiting to give his note to the teller, he began to worry that someone had seen him write the note and might call the police before he could reach the teller window. So he left the Bank of America and crossed the street to Wells Fargo.

After waiting a few minutes in line, he handed his note to the Wells Fargo teller. She read it and surmised from his spelling errors that he was not the brightest light in the harbor or the sharpest knife in the drawer. She told the would-be robber that she could not accept his stick-up note because it was written on a Bank of America deposit slip and that he would have to either fill out a Wells Fargo deposit slip or go back to the Bank of America.

Looking somewhat defeated, the man said, "Okay," and left the bank and headed back across the street. The Wells Fargo teller then called the police, who arrested the man a few minutes later, as he was waiting in line back at the Bank of America.

Another bank robber, in Bumpis, Tennessee, handed a teller the following note: "Watch out. This is a rubbery. I have an oozy traned on your but. Dump the money in a sack, this one. No die pakkets or other triks or I will tare you a new naval. No kwarter with red stuff on them, too." The teller started laughing, and the man fled the bank in embarrassment and with no booty.

In both instances, we note the relationship between bad spelling and incompetent commission of a felony. Dr. Creon V. B. Smyk, of the Ohio Educational Council, says such notes are, lamentably, the rule. "Right across the board, we see poor prewriting skills, problems with omissions, tense, agreement, spelling, and clarity," he moans.

Smyk believes that the quality of robbery notes could be improved if criminals could be taught to plan before writing. "We have to stress organization. Make an outline of your robbery note before you write it," he said. "Some of the notes get totally sidetracked on issues like the make, model, and caliber of the gun, number of bullets, etc., until one loses sight of the main idea—the robbery."

Spellos are especially embarrassing when perpetrated by those who are paid to know better. Winners of the Yellowstone County Spelling Bee, in Montana, received awards congratulating them on their SPEILLING. Organizers had the plaques redone to correct the spelling of SPELLING. A sign in front of a school identified the place as "Bridgeton High School—Where Excellance is a Tradition." Another sign identified the "College of Continueing Education and Community Service."

Classified ads have included:

- WANTED: Editors and proff readers
- Reeding tutors needed

- Full-service printer. A commitment to excellence.
- Experienced editor will edit manuscripts for substance, style, grammer, & punctuation.
- "The Monitor" reserves the right to edit letters for spelling, grammer, and punctuation, as well as possibly libelous material.
- Professionals will handle essays, term papers, research reports, and resume's.

Misspellings can end up screaming to the world in 18-point type, in part because homophones skillfully elude (not allude) the clutches of computerized spellcheckers:

NEW VACCINE MAY CONTAIN RABBIS

⊚

GIRLS SEEK BIRTHS ON U.S. TRACK TEAM

⊚

POLICE TO REWARD HELMETED
BIKERS, ROLLERBLADDERS

⊚

SENATE PANEL AGREES TO MUCH SEX ON TELEVISION

⊚

LOCAL MAN ARRESTED FOR
POSSESSION OF HEROINE

America has a long tradition of bad spelling. George Washington, reporting a shortage of provisions, wrote, "With respect to the Flower we find our Necessaties are not such as to require an immediate Transportation during the Harvist." He wrote "flagg" for *flag*, "ingagement" for *engagement*, and "centry" for *sentry*. President Andrew Jackson once blew his stack while trying to compose a presidential paper. "It's a damned poor mind that can think of only one way to spell a word," he thundered. Vice President Dan Quayle was widely ridiculed for having told a schoolchild that *potato* was spelled "potatoe." This glorious tradition of aberrant spelling continues unstinted:

- My father received a letter by special devilry.
- Now Hillary Rodham Clinton has returned, a kinder, gentler first lady, her tarnished halo residing over her well-coffered head.
- We are proud to inform you that you have been nominated for the helicopter heroism award. Do to your outstanding cat like in stinks, we feel that you are a shoe in against other nominees.
- Yes, this is the uncensored copy of Paula Jones's case against Bill Clinton—replete with details of Bill's sorted sexual advances.
- *In a restaurant review:* A fine meal here won't cost you a nominal egg.
- *From an east Texas Cable Company:* Please bare with us while we are working to improve service.
- *In the laundry room of an apartment complex:* Do not use washing machines for dying.
- $30 Water Pearl Neckless. $50 (and up) Bracelet & Neckless.
- WANTED: Job as janitor. Long experience. Expert moper.
- Local club needs experienced kook to run kitchen.
- The ship is lifted through a series of ingenuous locks.
- Marital Arts Studio
- Do not mumble. Annunciate your words clearly.
- UNC's Novac claims he never accussed anybody of a racial slur.
- I am opening a organic pet supply store in N.Y. and am looking for home bread puppies. Please contact me if you have any information about home bread puppies in my area.
- You are invited to Sally Curtis's retirement party. No gifts, just the honor of your presents.
- The company will decide whether or not to recognize same-sects marriages.
- For the prom I gave my date a boot and ear of roses.
- She had been really sick and fell into a comma for six months.
- The boy peddled his bicycle from South Dennis to Yarmouth.
- Please remember, Feed the Hungry needs any nonparishable food.

- The contractor shall provide uninformed police officers for traffic control.
- We need candid photos for the yearbook. Only decent pictures will be excepted.
- Sex should not be aloud.
- Dennis Tierney has studied the various voices, and rather than imitating the exact sounds of the character, he captures quirks and subtitles in their speech patterns.

Gleaming out among True Tales of Embarrassing Spellos is this gem from a newsletter serving a small town in Cape Cod, Massachusetts: The wife of the local rabbi was hired as a nursery school assistant. The newsletter announced the hiring with a paragraph that ended, "We are lucky to have Ruth joining Christine this year. Ruth will bring her lovely gentile manner to the classroom."

THE SPELLBOUND HALL OF FAME

- I have been raising this question for some years, but it is like the tree that falls in the dessert: Nobody hears it.
- In Pittsburgh, they manufacture iron and steal.
- ESCAPEE CAPTURED AFTER TEN DAYS ON THE LAMB
- Joan of Arc was burnt to a steak.
- They gave William IV a lovely funeral. It took six men to carry the beer.
- Grace Varney's voice broke with emotion as she clutched her toe-headed daughter as her son clung to her side.

The report was signed by five faulty members of the university.

An Embarrassment of Typos

In Ontario, Canada, man left the snow-filled streets of Toronto for a vacation in Florida. His wife was on a business trip and was planning to meet him there the next day.

When he reached his hotel, he decided to send his wife a quick e-mail. Unable to find the scrap of paper on which he had written her e-mail address, he did his best to type it from memory.

Unfortunately, he missed one letter, and his note was directed instead to an elderly woman whose husband had passed away only the day before. When the grieving widow checked her e-mail, she took one look at the monitor, let out a piercing scream, and fell to the floor in a dead faint. At the sound, her family rushed into the room and saw this note on the screen:

Dearest Wife:
> *Just got checked in. Everything prepared for your arrival tomorrow.*
>> *Your loving husband*
P.S. It sure is hot down here.

The English language is made to order for typographical errors and typographical terrors. That's because of the vast number of words whose meanings can be radically altered by the addition, omission, or transposition of a single character.

Each member of the U.S. Senate who signed in as "juror" for the historic impeachment trial of President Bill Clinton received as a souvenir the pen he or she had used. Each pen bore the words "Untied States Senator."

American writer Bret Harte once wrote in a California newspaper that a resident named Mrs. Callison "has long been known for her charity." The typesetter inadvertently altered the sentence to "has long been known for her chastity." The proofreader then put a question mark on the galley so that the typesetter would check the original copy.

The item came out in the newspaper thus: "Mrs. Callison has long been known for her chastity(?)."

A baby announcement in the *Gloversville* (N.Y.) *Morning Herald* concluded with an unfortunate sentence that showed how the inadvertent substitution of a single letter can completely reverse meaning: "The happy parents have the congratulations of all on this suspicious event."

Students heading back to class got a big surprise in Hendersonville, Florida. The new student handbook included a blunder that caught students and parents by surprise. It listed a particularly harsh punishment for "profanity—profane language will not be tolerated. Stern discipline will be death to any student guilty of this conduct." *Death*, of course, should have read *dealt*. With eerie similarity, a profile of Allston, Massachusetts, included a macabre listing of high schools: "Jackson Mann and Thomas Gardiner elementary schools, Horace Mann School for the Dead and Hard of Hearing."

"Red disk icon and contour bottle are trademarks of the Coca-Cola Company"—that was the text of a sticker plastered over a typographical error on promotional boxes of the soft drink. The "s" in the second word had erroneously appeared as a "c." The same Freudian slip was showing when a certain company advertised an "LS120 Floppy Drive: 120 MB dick space. Five times faster than 1.44 MB floppy"!

Have a look at some more typochondriacal headlines:

POLL SAYS THAT 53 PERCENT BELIEVE
MEDIA OFFEN MAKE MISTAKES

⊚

CLARK APPOINTED PUBIC RELATIONS
DIRECTOR AT SMU

⊚

COUNCIL EXPLORES PUTTING
COMMUNITY CENTER ON BROAD

⊚

INFANT MORALITY SHOWS DROP HERE

⊚

SEX CANDLES PLAGUE POLITICIANS

⊚

SUES BRIDE OF FOUR MOUTHS

⊚

HOTEL BURNS. 200 GUESTS
ESCAPE HALF GLAD

⊚

GRAHAM COUPLE IS ENTERTAINED
ON 50TH WEDDING

⊚

UNEASY CLAM SETTLES OVER MICHIGAN

◎

MANY MAINE WOMEN LIVE UNDER
THE TREAT OF DOMESTIC VIOLENCE

◎

SOCKS LOWER IN TOKYO

◎

WOMEN COMPROMISE 26 PERCENT
OF TOWN'S WORKERS

◎

LITERACY VOLUNTEERS COMBATS
PROBLEM OF ILLERACY

◎

ARE YOUNG AMERICANS
BE GETTING STUPIDER?

Have you heard about the hypochondriac who tested every medical cure in a famous digest magazine—and died of a typographical error? Here are the serendipitous findings of typochondriacs around the globe:

• *Entrapment,* starring Sean Connery and Catherine Zeta-Jones, is a terrific flick with two entertaining stars out doing themselves to keep our attention and on the edge of our seats.
• The report was signed by five faulty members of the university.
• No governor for many years has been able to love on the salary paid him.
• Christiansen was a foundering editor and associate publisher of *Food Arts* magazine.
• The centerway lot will follow the pattern of other lots as far as parking fees are concerned. The meters will permit parking for ten dents per hour.

- The president, who has been sick for several days, is now in bed with a coed.
- New technology relives the agony of severe low back and leg pain.
- From the end of her street, beauty consultant Janet Walker could clearly see the church where she was to parry trainee accountant Jared Gregg.
- Each evening will consist of a four-curse menu.
- Expectant mothers are urged to consume 400 mg daily of frolic acid.
- A recipe for beef tenderloin in the *Washington Post* "Food" section included "two pounds baby, stems removed and discarded."
- Dairy Queen seeking person w/ supervisory and fat food restaurant experience
- The open lot between the Walnut and Market St. bridges will be used for public fatherings on the river walk.
- VIEW! VIEW! VIEW! Price reduced on this beautiful custom townhouse built in 1992 in best part of Cardiff. Walking distance to beach. Good ocean view from most rooms plus duck on top has breathtaking views to the north & south. The perfect home for the entertainer.
- LEGAL SECRETARIES

Our firm is searching for two experienced litigational legal secretaries. Candidates must have two-to-five years of civil litigation experience and excellent organizational skills. Must also be a team layer, computer literate and type 65–70 wpm.
- Tomorrow we may expect strong northwest winds reaching a gal in exposed places.
- Advanced Life Painting Studio. This group grows out of a need for professional artists to have an opportunity to paint from the model. Tuition includes model feel.
- Ms. Dwyer has been raising birds for many years and is credited with having the largest parateets in the state.
- Her chrysanthemums in the autumn are a subtle joy; her lips in the spring are thrilling.
- The form for people who were making presentations at the 1998 meeting of the National Association of Student Personnel Administrators asked them to "Please Type or Print Legibly."

- SM, 36, professional, financially/emotionally secure, seeking SWF, 22–38, who likes to travel and experience different vultures.
- They were married and lived happily even after.
- The new Miss America will be drowned later before a nationwide television audience.
- Leasing agent, part-time. Applicants must have strong sales background, excellent telephone skills, and lost of enthusiasm.
- Mr. Ballard, who has been very ill the past week, is still under the car of Dr. Goldman.
- In a letter from a summer camp director: Dear Parents: We are pleased to announce the opening of registration. We are working hard and looking forward to the ultimate bummer experience.
- *In an obituary*: He also leaves tight grandchildren.
- HELP WANTED: Law firm needs secretary. Excellent benefits, including tension.
- Widows made to order. Send us your specifications.
- Women's Elf-Defense Class Scheduled
- A Census Bureau report revealed today that Southern girls do marry at an early urge.
- Nothing brightens the garden like primrose pants!
- Hooked on Phonies: great for any age!
- As an encore, Miss Brown played the old favorite "Carry Me Back to Old Virginity."
- The Kingston Gladiators Drum and Bungle Corps is seeking new members.
- The House of Representatives complied by voting enough funds to hide 15 additional state troopers.
- *In a personals column*: Josephine, please take me back. It was just a passing fanny. Your George
- A skunk was found wandering among the phews of one of the town's churches.
- They think that nothing matters except that they thrill to each other's ouch, and they never doubt but that they will go on billing and cooing forever.
- James and Phoebe Cummings celebrated their 50th anniversary on May 26. They renewed their rows at St. Patrick's Cathedral.

- Dip your soiled face in alcohol, rinse it in the liquid, and hang it out to dry. It may then be pressed.
- Join a friendly professional team at Newport Hospital. Various 8, 10 & 12 hour shits are available. Excellent benefits package.
- Theses and dissertations: A quick guide to writhing in the social and physical sciences
- *On an order coupon:* Send no money now. You will be bilked later.
- *In a campus housing pamphlet for Walla Walla College:* Under special circumstances, single students under age 23 may apply to the vice president for student administration for permission to love off campus.
- Former nursing aide Gerald Lebow has been sentenced to pay $15 a month for flowers sent weekly to Willows Nursing Home for 20 years. It's part of his sentence for sexually touching a female under his car.
- Most men make the mistake of not washing their faces thoroughly with hot soup and water before they begin shaving.
- *From a recipe:* Mix ingredients and form into a oaf.
- She is employed as an athletic strainer by the University of the South.
- If we would only send young American tenors to stud abroad, they would return immensely improved.
- He heard himself assailed as a self-centered financial executive who buttered his own beard.
- The bride collapsed killing five people.
- Social notes: He is visiting our town with the bitter half.
- Many diabetic children learn quickly how to give themselves injections. Almost all are skilled in the procedure by the time they are tight.
- There are millions of desirable women who are unattacked and hungry for love.
- Mr. and Mrs. Chester Lynes, of Philadelphia, are pictured here in Delphi, Greece, where they exploded antiques.
- A jury awarded the family $1.5 million in compensatory damages and $10 million in punitive damages. After deducting attorney's fees and expenses, the family received $4.96 in punitive damages, with the father recovering half and the children splitting the difference.

THE TYPO-GRAPHIC HALL OF FAME

- An in-debt discussion of the new tax laws is available by using the order blank in the tax return package.
- He received his graduate degree in unclear physics.
- During the current fiscal year, Kinney plans to increase the number of un-informed sergeants to a total of 42.
- It is said that there are more golf curses per square mile in North Carolina than anywhere else in the world.
- Now Playing: OKLAHOMO!
- THE "TRIBUNE" GAVE ME
  FAST SERVICE
  AND GREAT RESLUTS!
- Porpoises converse in complicated patterns of whistles, clivkd, sdsvsn mimiu dporka lsnhushrd.